# Praise for **Walk**

"This is a book by two free men—two men who have consciously chosen to forsake the desperate quest for speed that characterizes our increasingly impatient age in favor of long, slow, discursive rambles on foot over hill and dale, mountain and meadow, crag and creek and country road. Among other things, to walk in the way that Michael Perkins and Will Nixon do is an act of devotion, an act that entails a close reading of the landscape—and happily for us, they write as well as they read."
    —Mikhail Horowitz, *Rafting into the Afterlife*

"The writing is crisp and inviting, and the mix of current detail and historical anecdotes will keep readers interested. For me, it was just plain old fun to dip into."
    —Edward Sanders, *America: A History in Verse*

"Michael Perkins and Will Nixon step out into the Catskill mountains. They read the landscape like a book, and hold it open for us, wild and accessible, and invite us into the crags and balsams, the splendorous views. Their enthusiasm is catchy. We drink big gulps of the morning air without ever leaving our armchair."
    —Janine Pommy Vega, *The Green Piano*

"Henry David Thoreau once called walking the Fourth Estate—the other three were Church, State, and (here you have to smile) People. The implication is clear: if you want to get free of the burdens that weigh upon your mind, free of the kinds of obligations that only seem to multiply the more you fulfill them, and finally...even free of yourself, then go for a walk! *Walking Woodstock* is the perfect guidebook to America's first alternative religion and her oldest, most venerable revolutionary act. Read it as a natural history of the local flora and fauna (including the human variety), as the record of an evolving friendship between kindred souls, or as a personal challenge to wear out your next pair of shoes."
    —Clark Strand, *How to Believe in God:*
    *Whether You Believe in Religion or Not*

"Like Johnny Cash, Perkins and Nixon have been everywhere—through, over, under and around Woodstock, and not just Woodstock, New York. These bright remembrances of hikes past should inspire the couch-bound to retake the neglected territory of the upright and bipedal. There's wilderness, poetry and history in this Woodstock, a realm of mountain paths through winding glens and up windy slopes to hidden vistas, a back 40 peopled with the ghosts of Woodstockers past—settlers, sculptors, painters, quarrymen, Indian chiefs, town supervisors and more. No more informed, energized, cantankerous and amiable company could be found than these two foot soldiers of field and stream. Let them guide you where they go. And feel free to follow in their footsteps."

—Spider Barbour, *Wild Flora of the Northeast*

"*Walking Woodstock* is a graceful and honest book written with a poet's keen appreciation for the beauty that surrounds us and the deep pleasure of experiencing our highways and byways afoot. A story of friendship, companionship, and mutual respect—a lovely duet."

—Kenneth Wapner, *Catskill Rambles*

"Will Nixon and Michael Perkins have given us the next best thing to being out there: an interior trek through their imaginations, all the while following their instincts that lead them to the roads once taken, now enveloped by time and change. This eloquent, often poignant volume mirrors the very object of their pursuit: a lacework of connections, to people living on the forest edge, to generations past, present and future, to the sounds and smells and sights of the wild heart of the Catskills, and to hints of how life in Woodstock once was lived."

—Michael DeWan, Former President, Woodstock Land Conservancy

"These rambles of discovery around historic Woodstock will inspire you to depart the malls and walls and rediscover the natural world with new eyes. The prose is often lyrical: 'I found in front of my face a mossy bird's nest packed into a small cliff pocket like a woven throne.' Several stories recount in fascinating detail adventures in the Catskill mountains, and 'Lost' is one of the best tales of disorientation I've yet read."

—Carol White, *Catskill Day Hikes for All Seasons*

# Walking Woodstock

## Journeys into the Wild Heart
## of America's Most Famous Small Town

*To Marianna,*
*Thank you for joining us!*
*May these journeys inspire journeys of*
*your own!*

*Best wishes,*
*Will Nixon*

### Michael Perkins and Will Nixon

Acknowledgments

*The Woodstock Times* published many of these essays, sometimes in early versions. An abridged version of "Circumnavigation@3500" appeared in *The Catskill Canister*, the newsletter of the Catskill 3500 Club. *The Country and Abroad* published "Sold." "Lost" appeared online in *Half Moon Review*, then in *Catskill Peak Experiences*. "Fire Tower" appeared in *Adirondack Peak Experiences*.

Walking Woodstock : Journeys into the Wild Heart of America's Most Famous Small Town / Michael Perkins and Will Nixon.
[Woodstock, NY] : Bushwhack Books, 2009.
p. : ill. ; cm.
1. Walking-New York (State)-Ulster County-Guidebooks. 2. Hiking-New York (State)-Ulster County-Guidebooks. 3. Woodstock (N.Y.)- Guidebooks.
917.47

Illustrations by Carol Zaloom
Book Design and Typography by Melissa Mykal Batalin.

Printed by The Troy Book Makers in Troy, NY on recycled, acid-free paper.
www.thetroybookmakers.com

ISBN-13: 978-1-935534-39-6

In Memoriam

Linda Gabriel

Emma Segal

# A Note to the Reader

These essays are meant to entertain and inspire, not to provide detailed route directions. If trail maps exist for the route you'd like to walk, please use them. If guidebooks describe the trip, please consult them. And please respect the rights of private landowners.

The authors express their own opinions in these essays, not those of any organizations or other individuals. The authors are responsible for any errors that may appear.

Like many pleasurable activities hiking entails some risks. No one sets forth on a walk to get lost or be injured. Yet such things happen, as readers will learn in these pages. In such situations, when the sense of fear can be overwhelming, there is no substitute for being properly prepared with a map and compass, first aid kit, and other emergency supplies.

Please enjoy these journeys. May they lead to journeys of your own. While the risks of hiking are real, the rewards are the satisfactions of connecting with nature as well as oneself. Walking may seem a slow way to travel compared to the automobile, but it is a quick way to reach the soul. On foot we live life at its fullest.

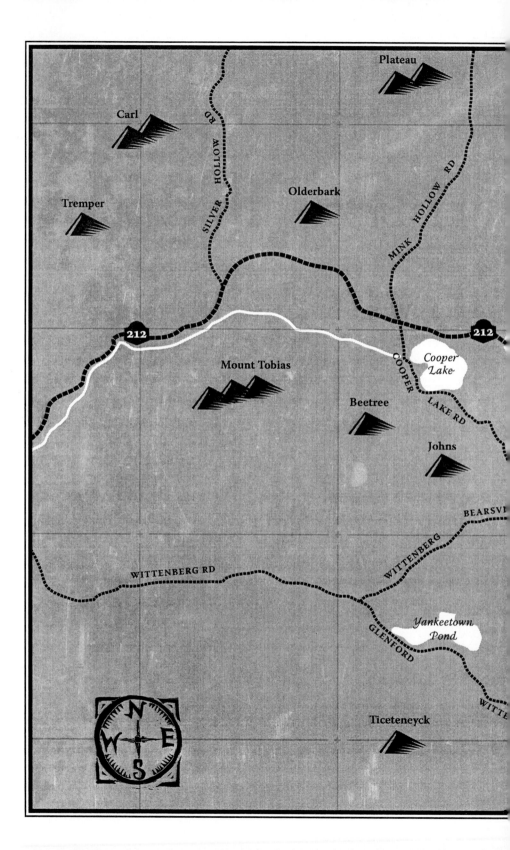

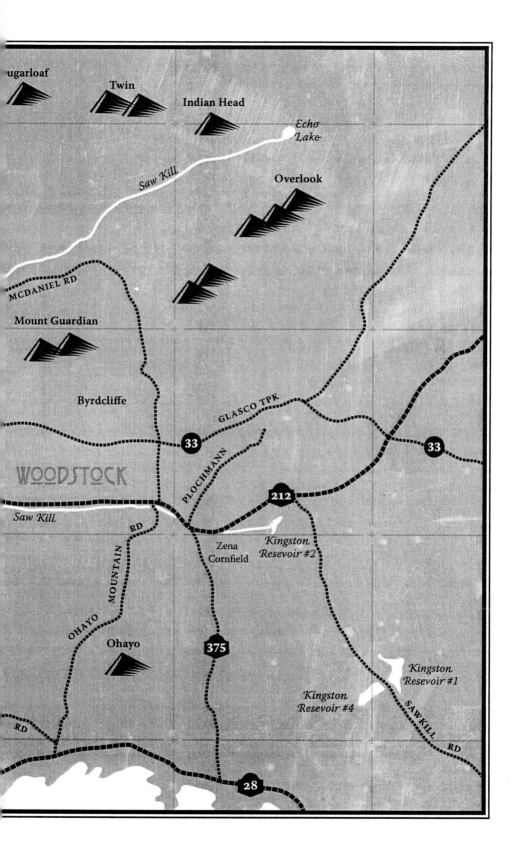

# Contents

## The Greater Catskills:
## Lost and Found in the Blue Mountains

## Wandering Thoughts and Sunbaked Opinions

## Overlook Mountain

"You are eligible to any good fortune when you are in the condition to enjoy a walk. When the air and water taste sweet to you, how much else will taste sweet! When the exercise of your limbs affords you pleasure, and the play of your senses upon the various objects and shows of nature quickens and stimulates your spirit, your relation to the world and to yourself is what it should be—simple and direct and wholesome. The mood in which you set out on a spring or autumn ramble or a sturdy winter walk, and your greedy feet have to be restrained from devouring the distances too fast, is the mood in which your best thoughts and impulses come to you, or in which you might embark upon any noble and heroic enterprise. Life is sweet in such moods, the universe is complete, and there is no failure or imperfection anywhere."

—John Burroughs

# Declaration of Independence

Michael Perkins

THERE ARE MANY REASONS for taking a walk, and virtue is the least of them. If you step forth on a fine September morning with any motivation other than to be selfishly footloose and fancy-free for an hour or two, chances are that you're the kind of pedestrian soul who participates in those group charity marches known as "walkathons" and who hopes perambulating around the mall before the shops open is "heart healthy." You deserve merit badges for these efforts, because of course there's virtue galore in good works and staying alive, but if you were to tell the truth, you'd rather be driving. Your right foot itches not for a hill to climb, but to put the pedal to the metal.

The sole motivation that will keep you walking for a lifetime is freedom. Taking a walk is a declaration of independence, like unhooking from the grid, or shooting your television, as that desert walker Edward Abbey once did. Walking is subversive. If you're a road walker like me, you will find out just how subversive. Drivers speed past you in deadly weapons that kill thirty-five hundred a month in the U.S., jeering and laughing because they assume you're either too dumb or too poor to join their rat race.

One of the beauties of going for a walk is how little equipment you need. A pair of comfortable but sturdy shoes, a hat to shield you from the sun, rain, and cold, some water and maybe a snack. A walking stick is essential, but one can be had for the looking on any forest floor. A stick offers the third leg you sometimes need to propel you up hills and brake your descent, and since occasionally you meet dogs who resist your passing through their territory, it may come in handy as an anklebiterknocker. (And if you're one of those sentimental saps who believes that Rover should run free, I'll tell you about all the great dogs I've befriended on my walks whose lives were cut short by cars.)

I must confess that I also drive. Although I try to avoid the experience—as do people who've had the misfortune to ride with me—I'm sometimes spotted on the local roads braking for paper bags and otherwise acting like Mr. Magoo. But mostly, I walk three and a half miles over a mountain to get to work. Daily, I charge up Ohayo Mountain—and the operative word is "charge!" like Teddy Roosevelt is supposed to have charged up San Juan Hill in the Spanish-American war. You stab your stick into the pavement, your breath rasps in your throat, your thighs burn, and up up up you go. To the sedentary, this doubtlessly sounds masochistic, and in many ways it is.

But at the top of the mountain you catch your breath, smile as the endorphins kick in, and find that you're...happy. As if you're in a movie musical, you look around for a bluebird to tell this to, or Jiminy Cricket. You proceed, at a good clip, looking at things as you go in a new way. Because you have the freedom to stop and look, you see the landscape for the first time. (The English poet W. H. Davies got it right when he wrote in a poem entitled "Leisure" the following Deep Thought: "What is this life if, full of care/We have no time to stand and stare.")

Walking freely along stimulates thought processes you don't ordinarily have access to. I think of them as Open Road thoughts. They are expansive and hopeful. Everything seems possible. After all, if you can push yourself over a mountain, you begin to think that you can do anything. Thus forced marches are still a part of military training, even though soldiers drive to war in Humvees. Smart corporations would give bonuses to employees who walked to work.

But don't get so absorbed in your thoughts that you neglect safety. Always walk facing traffic. Face the danger, don't let it sneak up on you from behind. Wear something bright at all times, especially at night, when you should carry a flashlight. Heed the warning of road kill.

Although the basic motivation for going for a walk should be freedom, there's a lot to be said for having a destination in mind, or an errand to fulfill. Anything that gets you out of the car. Any excuse, even virtue, will do.

Since walking is even more addictive than driving, you'll want to do it even when the weather is threatening. The real walker ventures forth despite rain, snow, heat, or high water. Carry a poncho, and remember that an umbrella makes a good walking stick. Cars will stop occasionally and offer you a ride. On a fine day, if you're not late for an appointment, politely decline these invitations. On a rotten weather day, I'm likely to accept a ride more often than not; I meet my neighbors and make new friends.

When I started walking over twenty years ago, I had no idea of where it might lead. But my walks got longer and longer. One year I walked from Red Hook in Dutchess County to Pittsfield, Massachusetts, via road and trail, in homage to Herman Melville, whose house, Arrowhead, is outside Pittsfield. In 1986, to publicize the Woodstock Bicentennial, I walked from Woodstock's Village Green to the Village Green of Woodstock, Connecticut— across the state—in one week.

It's obvious that walking can make you crazy, in a good kind of way. It teaches you that you can be free, at least for an hour or so a day, if you want to be—that all you have to do is hit the road, Jack or Jill, to change your life.

# The Last Radical Act Left in Woodstock

Will Nixon

IN MY FIRST MONTHS IN WOODSTOCK, I decided that I'd found the last radical act left in this famous but graying bastion of the Sixties, namely, walking. I arrived in November fresh from a long stay in the Adirondacks, where I'd finished the Adirondack Forty-Sixers in a surge of hiking that got me into my best shape in ages. Not wanting to become a winter potato, I took a walk almost every day. The problem was that I rarely made it out of the house before dark. As a writer, I had the luxury (or curse) of sitting at the computer all day in my bathrobe and long johns, writing (or deleting) until I'd worn out my brain by five or six in the evening. Then I'd pull on my jeans, lace up my boots, zip up my fleece, grab my hat and gloves, find my flashlight, and head out my cottage door to explore the village lanes and woodsy cul-de-sacs of my new home terrain.

In 1996 I'd left midtown Manhattan for a log cabin at the edge of the wilderness in Phoenicia. I could climb up the steep slope of hemlocks behind my cabin and keep going to the summit of Panther Mountain without seeing a soul, passing only a hunter's shack on the way. I had the perfect setup: a wood stove and a front porch perched like a tree fort above my stream. Never again, I promised myself, would I be so confined by civilization that I couldn't step outside my front door to pee.

So much for promises. Eight years later I felt just as lucky to find a village rental. By then, I'd tired of the country driving that ate up my days. I happily traded the wood stove for a wall thermostat. And Woodstock was that rare community designed for walking. I celebrated my first morning by doing something I hadn't done since 1996 in midtown: I walked out to breakfast. How civilized not to hop in the car every time I needed groceries or a cappuccino fix. As an environmentalist, I was the proud owner of a Honda Insight, a hybrid that averaged fifty-three miles per gallon. But in the village, I discovered an alternative better than hybrids, namely, not driving at all.

For my evening exercise, I developed several routes around side streets and cul-de-sacs. To walk in the village at night is to be a voyeur who can see into the brightly lit homes of people going about ordinary lives, such as a woman at a kitchen counter or a man seated with a newspaper in front of a TV. I stood out under the stars, wrapped in warm clothes, enjoying the nighttime expansiveness, yet I felt surprisingly touched by these scenes of domestic warmth and belonging. I remembered John Cheever's stories about outsiders who longed to fit into the suburbs. But I'd grown up in the suburbs and vowed never to move back. I was proud of not having mowed a lawn since pre-Ronald Reagan. Walking past ranch houses indulged my nostalgia for my suburban upbringing without forcing me to enter the door.

But I also wanted exercise. I didn't want to lose what I'd gained by conquering the Adirondack Forty Sixers. Leaving the flats, I rounded the bend at the base of Ohayo Mountain Road and ascended the long steep straightaway that gave me the StairMaster experience. My heartbeat sped up. I pulled off my hat and gloves to stay cool. I waved my flashlight wildly at cars charging down this roadway that wasn't built for pedestrians. Forget about sidewalks. In places I had inches between the pavement and hedges. Yet the cars always saw me and swerved wide. I tried not to think about Stephen King, a walker like many writers, who'd been hit by a drunk on a country highway in broad daylight, landing him in the hospital for months. But I wasn't Stephen King. I didn't have his talent, his success, or his fame. Why should I have his accident?

In time I realized that I never saw anyone else out on foot. Even the Lefties drove by. I decided that I was committing the last radical act left in the age of petroleum man: walking. Flashlight in hand, I returned down Ohayo Mountain Road, self-righteous and charged up on endorphins. I may have missed the famous Sixties protests, but I was out here marching night after night.

Doing my part to slow global warming. I studied the gaudy constellation of mountainside lights across the valley on Overlook and amused myself by coming up with an insulting names like the Big Zipper.

In the spring I discovered Plochmann Lane. It became my favorite, an idyllic road that began among ranch houses, continued through forest where driveways led to hidden houses, and finished beside meadows with wonderful views of Overlook Mountain. The perfect route, providing a blend of exercise and pastoral scenery. It also disabused me of my fantasy of being the only walker in town. I met people strolling with friends or dogs. Occasionally, my friends, who happened to be driving by, stopped to stay hello. Through Match.com I met a woman who lived on Plochmann Lane. We dated for a few months, taking walks of our own.

By spring I also recognized the people who walked by my cottage on Pine Grove Street. There was the waiter from New World Home Cooking who gently tugged his tiny dog on a leash from shrub to shrub. The racewalker swinging her elbows like weapons; she turned out to be a writer I'd met in my earlier life in Manhattan. The mailman was an inveterate walker, a lanky fellow in blue mailman shorts pushing his cart down the street. But the one who intrigued me was Michael Perkins, a tall thin man with stooped shoulders who looked frail with his walking stick yet floated along on his feet. Years earlier, he'd written a glowing review of my first poetry chapbook for the *Woodstock Times*, for which I remained eternally grateful. But I couldn't say I knew him well. He worked at the library. He lived on the other side of Ohayo Mountain. Now I realized that he was walking to and from work. He was commuting on foot, more than three miles each way. He truly was the alternative to petroleum man.

One evening we met with a third fellow to drink red wine, sample fine cheeses, and read Hart Crane aloud. A difficult poet from the 1920's, famous for writing an epic inspired by the Brooklyn Bridge as well as for jumping off a ship to kill himself at age thirty-two, Crane was a figure generally ignored today. But we were fans. We knew that Crane had stayed for two months on Plochmann Lane in the 1920's, where he'd enjoyed a festive Thanksgiving with John Dos Passos and painters from the arts colony. In fact, Michael shared a short play with us that he'd written about this gathering. Like Crane, Michael had grown up in Ohio but moved to Manhattan as a young man to make his way in the world of literature. As a young poet, Michael had paid homage to Crane by walking across the Brooklyn Bridge while reciting long passages of "The Bridge" from memory. That impressed me. I'd never memorized more than a handful of sonnets, much less one of the most challenging long poems in American literature.

And Michael had done more, a lot more. In honor of Herman Melville, he'd once walked from Red Hook on the other side of the Hudson to Arrowhead, Herman Melville's house in the Berkshires. To celebrate Woodstock's bicentennial he'd walked from our town to Woodstock, Connecticut in 1986, a four-day journey on roads. Though I'd met countless hikers in the Catskills and the Adirondacks, I'd never met anyone like Michael, a man who really had taken his own path in life. "Who is this guy?" I thought. "And how do I get to walk with him?"

|||||||||||||||||||||||||||||||||||||||||||||||||||||||||||||||||||||||||||||||||||||||||||||||||
Plochmann Lane remains a favorite. Though I no longer live in the village, I sometimes drive into town just to walk it. I park at the Bradley Meadows shopping center, walk left at Playhouse Lane, swing right on Whites Lane, and finally turn left on Plochmann. Two miles from the start Plochmann ends at Glasco Turnpike. Often I turn around and walk back, though sometimes I turn left onto Glasco, then left onto Rock City Road for a four-mile loop back into the village. –W.N.
|||||||||||||||||||||||||||||||||||||||||||||||||||||||||||||||||||||||||||||||||||||||||||||||||

# A WALK ACROSS
# OLD WOODSTOCK

# Bewitched Pigs Dance on Their Noses in Mink Hollow, and a Whale Spouts in Cooper Lake: A True Report

Michael Perkins

COMES A WARM WEEKEND, and it's really spring at last. Time to limber up stiff winter legs and get out and about. So when stalwart hiker Will Nixon proposed that we walk across Woodstock, I jumped at the opportunity.

"Let's start at Mink Hollow," I said, "at the site of Captain Elias Hasbrouck's house on the corner of 212. That crossroads was called Little Shandaken in his time."

"Whoa. Back up. What are you talking about?" Will asked, reasonably enough.

I acknowledge a certain obsessiveness about local history. I explained that Captain Hasbrouck was a Revolutionary war hero, and Woodstock's first Supervisor. The first Woodstock Town Meeting and election was held at his house, which was situated at the entrance to the road over Mink Hollow, once a major thoroughfare to Tannersville and Greene County. Later home to artists, rock stars and movie royalty, Mink Hollow had been famous for its witches. Among the tricks they played, bewitching pigs so they danced on their noses was my favorite. I liked to imagine Captain Hasbrouck saddling up to ride into the hamlet down Shadwick's Lake Road, as Cooper Lake was called when the Shadwicks settled the area.

Will grinned amiably, and we proceeded to plan our epic hike. We would start at the historical marker at Little Shandaken and go by shank's mare down Cooper Lake Road looking for signs of spring, stopping at Bearsville. The first leg of our journey would be a stroll, a walk in the park. The second would be more challenging: to walk along the Sawkill from Bearsville to the Comeau. Our goal was to end up at Will's house in Zena—a symbolic destination chosen because Zena was the first settled part of Woodstock.

On the appointed April morning it was cool and foggy. We crossed 212 and started up Cooper Lake Road. Our first sign of spring was a ripped-open bag of garbage in the middle of the road. "Bear," Will said, conjecturing that the claw marks on a nearby telephone pole were also a sign of bruin. This was confirmed by a tall figure who came striding toward us. Tom takes his daily constitutional on the road, and according to him the bear crosses the road every morning between six and seven. When breakfast calls...

A little further on, we noticed an historical marker about the Down Rent Wars, when locals dressed as Indians made a violent protest against absentee landlords in 1844.

The morning sun was burning the fog off the lake. We saw two Canadian geese, and a red winged blackbird in a marsh where spider webs looking like cotton balls decorated bushes. Tiny golden coltsfoot poked up through the roadside gravel.

Then the expanse of the lake stretched before us, suddenly illuminated by full sun glinting on the water. It's an extraordinary sight, its beauty on a par with any landscape in Switzerland or the Sierras. As we stood there drinking in the view, Will noticed a geyser on the far side of the lake, water spouting: "Is that the famous Cooper Lake whale?" he asked. The morning was so magical I could even believe in dragons, forget about whales.

It was at that moment that we heard the thrilling, liquid cry of the Adirondacks: two loons flew over us making their music far from home.

Kingston owns Cooper Lake, and stands zealous guard over access to it. I recalled being able to walk freely on its shores in the 1980's. We'd gone skinny-dipping there on warm summer nights. No longer. Thus I was somewhat envious of the owners of the two houses that stand across the road from the lake's edge, the only houses on the road to command a panoramic view. Did they take advantage of their proximity on moonlit nights?

Because lakes are rare in the Catskills, Cooper Lake was one of the major scenic attractions in the nineteenth century. Alf Evers's *Woodstock: History of an American Town* tells us that in 1888 there were hopes that it would become a resort center. Summer people would come over Mink Hollow from Tannersville to enjoy the cooling waters. The combination of water, low mountains and tall pines was sublimely intoxicating.

A phoebe whistled as we climbed away from the lake and hit paved road, where stately old farmhouses and broad cultivated fields attested to early settlement.

Before we knew it, we had arrived in Bearsville, where Christian Baehr built his general store and where forty years ago a powerful music baron named Grossman put Bearsville on the international map, representing Bob Dylan and The Band.

Below the large windows of the Bear Cafe glistened the Sawkill, by which route we would hike into the hamlet on the next part of our search for spring in Woodstock.

The City of Kingston posts its reservoir lands around Cooper Lake. So long as you respect these signs, you won't find a prettier road walk in Woodstock. I park on Cooper Lake Road at the pullover at the eastern end of the lake. This road runs for a mile or so by the water. –W.N.

# Walking the Sawkill: Not a
# Gunshot to be Heard

Will Nixon

ON THE FIRST LEG of our walk across old Woodstock, Michael and I arrived at the Bearsville Post Office in fine shape. He hadn't even finished his snack pack of peanut butter crackers.

For the second leg we had grander ambitions. We'd follow the Sawkill from Bearsville into Woodstock. But we had trepidations. "My heritage is Kentucky, where people get shot for walking on other people's land," Michael said, when we met at the Post Office on another bright morning.

"But if we get shot, we make the front page," I said. It was my turn to chronicle our trek for the *Woodstock Times*.

Michael laughed. At least I hoped his chortle was a laugh.

Welcome to the great Catskills conundrum. Our region may be fabled for trout streams. But try to find one to walk beside for a morning. Our mountains have trails you can hike for days, but our valley streams flow through private lands. The Comeau property with its streamside trail is the rare exception. But Michael and I didn't want to hike Route 212 from Bearsville to the Comeau. We wanted to explore the Sawkill.

Behind the Bearsville Theater we paused at the memorial for Albert Grossman, the music impresario who died in 1986. A memorial boulder, honoring him as "the little bear," rested in a lawn corner past stone benches and ivy trimmed into an oval. Nearby, though, escaped ivy grew in wild patches amid brown forest leaves. Michael saw no signs of a path. We'd be trespassing for real.

We were immediately rewarded by the sight of our first fiddlehead fern of spring, a delicate sprout fuzzy with hair. A few steps farther we found Dutchman's breeches, an endearing little plant with flowers like billowy white pants hung on a laundry line. After our late crazy winter spring was bursting out. The bare trees had unfurled baby leaves. I treated Michael to a spicy leaf from a garlic mustard plant, a prolific weed shooting up faster than anything else around. "I haven't had this in years," Michael said, savoring the taste. "I like it."

Then he stopped. "House," he warned.

Through the scrim of trees we saw a low white building. In truth, we weren't afraid of getting shot. Dave Holden, the Comeau trail master, who knows the Sawkill well, had drawn a map and told us what to expect. (Dave has hiked the Sawkill from Echo Lake, its source, all the way to Kingston, which gives him a PhD in trespassing.) One homeowner, Dave had warned, was known to holler at people on her stream bank. But she wouldn't be armed. Still, we felt nervous. In our combined forty-five years in Woodstock neither Michael or I had tried the walk we were now undertaking.

A stone and dirt berm ran beside the stream. We scrambled over this barrier to get out of sight of the house and continued on the silt and stone stream bank by the shallow avenue of water flowing with white ripples. After skirting below someone's metal garden bench on the berm, we climbed up and followed this grassy embankment, which was like a rail trail without a trail. The forest now revealed nothing but trees. Looking back, I saw that the Bearsville Theater had vanished. Within minutes we'd slipped the bounds of the bucolic but man-made landscape to find ourselves by a wild stream. Our anxieties had passed. Now we could enjoy our discoveries.

On Route 212 the drive from Bearsville to Woodstock takes a few minutes on a straight road past meadows. Pretty but pastoral muzak. Not so for the Sawkill. The stream radically changes its personality every half mile. At first we had an easy time on raised banks beside the cobblestone stream. I was impressed by the sycamores, not a tree I associate with the Catskills, but then again how often do I walk in their streamside habitats? Their gray and green camouflage bark appeals to me, perhaps because of formative experiences with G.I. Joe dolls. But one granddaddy of a sycamore had bark like cracked river mud. I snapped Michael's picture beside the wide trunk as if he'd found an old-growth giant.

Across Yerry Hill Road we reentered the woods, but came to crushed gray rock poured far across the forest floor like the base for a cul-de-sac road. Had we stumbled into a construction site? Then, exiting to a sunny clearing for what we expected to be the Sawkill, we found instead a wide river channel made with this gray rock. It resembled a highway construction project without the guys in orange vests. A brown trickle of water lay in the bottom. Michael didn't like this human engineering one bit. "They've made the Sawkill look like a sewage channel," he said.

(Later, Mike Reynolds of the town highway department told me that this was an overflow channel built to cope with flooding that threatens several houses by the stream. The material spread in the forest filled in flood gullies.)

In a hundred yards we left this moonscape-like channel for the natural landscape of the Sawkill. But not the easy terrain we'd enjoyed upstream. No, we entered a battle zone created by flooding. Fallen trees blocked our way. A network of stone-bottomed trenches had been cut four feet deep through embankment soils. We weren't even sure where the Sawkill was. Yet we persisted, climbing over logs and navigating trenches, until we met the ultimate challenge: two small houses amid the trees at the creek bend.

"I see a parked car," Michael said. That settled matters. We left the stream and our intrepid bushwhack to find our way to Route 212 and the relative safety of walking on the shoulder beside traffic. We came out by Sunfrost. The high drama of the flood zone gave way to a blue sky and the sound of a lawn mower. Minutes later we sat on a guardrail for a canteen break. I heard my first catbird of spring, a long rapid musical burst that's both melodious and grating, a robin's song put through a grinder. But I've listened to enough avant-garde jazz to enjoy it.

For the final stretch we walked up Sled Hill to the Comeau. Past the soccer fields we entered the loop trail that Dave Holden

and others have maintained with loving care. No more butt sliding over downed trees. We enjoyed an idyllic streamside walk. To my surprise, Michael had never walked the full length of the loop.

He was enamored by the trail which had blazes and shipping pallets laid down to protect wet soil spots. "Dave Holden is hero of the hour," he said. In places ropes linked between trees like handrails helped us with the steep pitches.

The Sawkill had changed again. No more sycamores aching to leaf out in the sun. Now we walked under shady hemlocks. No more cobblestone streambed. Now the stream flowed though pools and over bedrock slabs, then poured down a waterfall with frothing white power. "This is beautiful," Michael said. "I've never been here before. Wow!"

The loop trail brought us out past the outdoor stage near the town offices. The moral of our hike, Michael said, was that walkers should advocate for English law under which we'd have a historic right to cross private fields. "I've walked across people's front lawns," Michael recalled of trips in England. "They come out and say, 'Hello, how are you?'" It seemed a shame that so much of the Sawkill should be off-limits to the public.

Despite our worries about trespassing, the only trouble of the morning came from my own foolishness. It's my theory that if you look hard enough you can find a golf ball almost anywhere. I've collected them miles from any golf course in Devil's Notch, Silver Hollow, etc. To my delight, I spotted a close relative, a plastic baseball laid as neatly as an egg in tangled roots low on the stream bank. To claim my souvenir, I got on my knees and leaned down to reach it. At that moment my pocket camera tucked in my shirt pocket slipped out to fall with a plunk into the stream, lost forever in the brown water.

"Oh, no!" Michael exclaimed.

What could I say? I'd been having fun photographing our walk for the newspaper. At least the camera was a disposable one so I was only out $20. And maybe the mishap was a blessing in disguise. Without meaning to, I'd dumped the photographic evidence that we'd ignored the "No Trespassing" signs to enjoy a magical morning by the Sawkill.

|||||||||||||||||||||||||||||||||||||||||||||||||||||||||||||||||||||||||||||||||||||||||||||||||||

The Comeau Property is the green heart of Woodstock. It has town offices, an outdoor stage for summer Shakespeare, soccer fields, and two miles of loop trails through the woods and alongside the Sawkill. The parking area is at the top of the long driveway on Tinker Street up to the town offices. –W.N.

|||||||||||||||||||||||||||||||||||||||||||||||||||||||||||||||||||||||||||||||||||||||||||||||||||

# Waghkonck Arrival

Michael Perkins

"THE LEAVES HAVE COME OUT since we started in Mink Hollow," Will
Nixon commented as we began the third leg of our walk across
Woodstock in search of spring. It was cold and overcast, as it had
been on that Mink Hollow morning; in three weeks we had, by following the Sawkill, followed the progress of a long, cool spring. Our
destination was Will's house on Sawkill Road just beyond Kingston
Reservoir Number One in Waghkonck, the Native American name
for the oldest part of Woodstock, called by us Zena.

Skipping the hamlet itself, and the golf course that was once
the Riseley Farm, we resumed our adventure at Big Deep, the
town swimming hole, notorious as a hippie *bagnio* in the Sixties.
Standing at the edge of the rocky pool in the silvery light, the
water gray, the sky gray, I flashed back to the faces of my children
as they emerged from the cold water in midsummer long ago.

In that ghostly light we set our boots on a path to Little Deep,
down the Sawkill. Walking on bluffs above the swiftly rushing
stream, we came to a marsh where we encountered two geese followed by three precision-swimming goslings. The fragrant morning air was filled with birdsong, and the hum of mosquitoes zero-
ing in on my neck.

We discovered an impressive old brick dam through which
a waterfall cut, and found, nearby, a manhole cover with a rusty
lock. "Could this be Woodstock's secret ICBM missile silo?" Will
wondered. A little further on we came upon an official facility
of prefab steel guarded by a chainlink fence. It was well tended
and unmarked, slightly sinister in the pearlescent light. Sure
enough, there was a sign that said this was a "NYS Permitted Dis-
charge Point"—doubtlessly where the Town Fathers and Mothers
(another sign told us we were on town property) leaked excess
community bile as a safety precaution.

By proceeding up hill and down dale we arrived at Little Deep, a series of swimming holes not as magical as Big Deep, perhaps, but surely refreshing, I mused, to the Indians, Dutch, English, and American farmers who labored in centuries past in the Zena Cornfield across the road.

We stood looking out over the twenty-two acres of field now under the protection of the Woodstock Land Conservancy. Alf Evers told me that Dutch fathers had begun growing crops on that Indian bottomland in 1720. Militias drilled there during the Revolution. The vast Zena Cornfield offers the best panoramic view of Overlook Mountain I know of, but this morning its summit was still shrouded by fog.

Just beyond the Cornfield is Gitnick Road. We decided to try it as a possible avenue to resuming our streamside walk, but it dead-ended into someone's yard, and I was not about to tiptoe through someone's tulips to gain access to the elusive Sawkill. I am faint-hearted about trespass.

So we kept to Zena Road, walking past the large field owned by the Downer family on the right, headed for the S curve where houses date back to 1750, and it occurred to me that I knew a kind soul there who might offer us a glimpse not only of the stream, but of what Zena must have looked like in its early days.

It was a long shot that Stella would be home, but there was a car in her driveway. I faced a minor dilemma: although I knew that Stella had the best view of the Sawkill on the road, I hesitated to knock because I don't like dropping in on people unannounced. You're likely to find out what they really think of you. So I called out her name politely, timidly; a trimmer. Fortunately, Will is made of sterner stuff. He stepped forward and rapped on the wooden door.

The door opened, and Stella peered quizzically out at us. When we explained our purpose, she graciously invited us to step out on to her deck which overlooks the Sawkill at one of its wildest points. We gazed down at a world class swimming hole

and a stone dam through which water rushed. Stella pointed out the bricked-over sluice gate in the dam. Her house had been a sawmill, here at a juncture where the water never stops rushing—indeed, it rises up from underground.

"The sound of water is so soothing," she told us, "and it drowns out the traffic noise." We were further treated to a look at her neighbor's house, which had been a grist mill until World War I.

To our disappointment, Stella told us it would be impossible to walk the Sawkill on her side of the stream. The banks were too steep.

So down the road we strode, stopping occasionally so Will could bring his binoculars to bear on a bird. Wild mustard sprinkled its white blossoms at our knees, and honeysuckle wafted its bouquet to our noses.

At the crossroad where Zena Road meets Sawkill Road and John Joy there is a blue historical marker put up in the 1930's telling us that the area was Waghkonck to the Indians, and Van Dale to English settlers. But it was the Dutch who were the first settlers, tenants from Kingston who were eventually able to buy their farms, sawmills and grist mills, people who crossed the Hudson on May Day to pay their rent in bushels of wheat to Madame Margaret Livingston at Clermont, who owned Van Daal. Looking around, we saw the Zena firehouse behind which is hidden Woodstock's oldest graveyard; the Tennis Club next to which stands the stone Van Etten House, once home to New World Home Cooking and a series of other eateries.

"You don't see anything when you rush by in a car," I declared, as we neared the limpid waters of Kingston Reservoir Number One. The reservoir has supplied water to Kingston since 1883. Starting at Cooper Lake and finishing at the reservoir, we had walked between two lakes owned by Kingston.

Will's binoculars flashed. He had spotted a merganser tooling through the water like the roadrunner. I didn't ask if it was a common merganser, a red breasted, or a hooded, but Will probably would have known.

Walking across Woodstock, taking the time to look at things, following the natural highway of the Sawkill, we had seen our home town in a fresh light. It demonstrated to me once again the primacy of bipedalism over most other means of enjoying life. See the world, make a new friend, slow down.

As we neared Will's house he pointed to a rare sight: a great blue heron lifting off from the water like a 747 aimed skyward.

‖‖‖‖‖‖‖‖‖‖‖‖‖‖‖‖‖‖‖‖‖‖‖‖‖‖‖‖‖‖‖‖‖‖‖‖‖‖‖‖‖‖‖‖‖‖‖‖‖‖‖‖‖‖‖‖‖‖
Big Deep is the town swimming hole. The turnoff isn't marked, but it's on Route 212 a mile east of the Village Green and just past Casablanca Road on the south side. The parking pullover for the short trail into Little Deep is on Zena Road about a quarter mile south of the turnoff from Route 212 onto Zena Road. Walk west into the woods to reach the swimming area. —W.N.
‖‖‖‖‖‖‖‖‖‖‖‖‖‖‖‖‖‖‖‖‖‖‖‖‖‖‖‖‖‖‖‖‖‖‖‖‖‖‖‖‖‖‖‖‖‖‖‖‖‖‖‖‖‖‖‖‖‖

# WOODSTOCK TO WOODSTOCK:

## A Bicentennial Journey

# Walking to Woodstock:
## Notes of a Tireless Pedestrian (1986)

Michael Perkins

ON AN OVERCAST COLUMBUS DAY morning I left the Woodstock Village Green with the good wishes of the steering committee of the Woodstock Bicentennial Celebration ringing in my ears, and started off on a four and a half day solo walk across northern Connecticut to Woodstock, Connecticut, tucked away in the quiet northeastern part of the Nutmeg State near the Massachusetts and Rhode Island borders.

I chose that classic New England village with the hometown name (instead of Woodstock, Vermont, or New Woodstock, New York, or any of the other one hundred and seventy Woodstocks in the world) because this year its citizens are celebrating their Tercentenary, and next year is Woodstock's Two Hundredth birthday as an incorporated township. I hoped that by walking between the sister towns I could attract some public attention to both celebrations of heritage, not to mention that the fall foliage would be peaking along the scenic routes I would follow, and I wanted to stretch my legs before winter.

Saugerties. Monday afternoon. The first fourteen miles from Woodstock to the Saugerties marina were a pleasant warm-up. I saw unexpected beauties I hadn't noticed in fifteen years of driving to Saugerties, like the nineteenth-century houses on the road leading down to the marina, where Eric Glass and three members of the Woodstock Youth Center were waiting to take me aboard the twenty-one-foot powerboat Eric owns with John LaValle. We sped down the middle of the choppy river, Billie Holiday singing, "As Time Goes By," and Eric put in neatly at the Rhinecliff train station dock. I lifted my bamboo staff in farewell to the mountains of Onteora, and strode off across Dutchess County, light-footed and light-hearted, walking again.

Salisbury, Conn. Monday evening. Arrived after dark, having walked hours in a light rain, feeling ever since leaving Millerton, on the New York border, that I'd crossed not simply into another state, but into another country called New England. The landscape was more sedate, the people more reserved, the quiet old villages more conscious of the past than their New York counterparts.

Every village I passed through had its white Congregational church with pedimented doorways and Palladian windows, and in every village the liveliest spot was the package liquor store. Religion, drink and history were the surface ingredients of public life, not—to my dismay at times—public lodging, public phones, or park benches for the weary. Nor were there tourists. I expected the White Hart Inn on the Salisbury town green to be full of leaf-followers, but the large old inn was nearly empty.

A plump bartender wiped glasses in the bar, waiting for the World Series crowd to arrive later. When her quiet oak domain was invaded by two local workmen in a flirtatious mood, I settled back in my chair to observe Connecticut courting habits. The older man's name was Gino. He was slender, dark and bearded, and determined to make Rosalind laugh by demonstrating that he could tie a cherry stem with his tongue. He succeeded in making her laugh, but she protested when he came behind the bar demanding that she pull the cherry from between his lips and see for herself.

Dinner was in a large nearly empty dining room, good food impeccably served. Near me a mother spoke to her prep school son in French while his English father lectured him about the Duke of Wellington and the stock market.

New Hartford. Tuesday night. Rain again, off and on through twelve hours of slogging through the lower Berkshire towns of Canaan, Norfolk and Winsted on Route 44 East. A late lunch in the Hawk's Nest Pub in Norfolk kept my spirits up and the sun emerged. I enjoyed the Englishness of the village, the beautiful library, spacious green, and historic white buildings, surrounded by low rolling hills forested with scarlet, gold and green masses of autumn color.

Winsted was the first mill town I passed through, at dinner time. On the map my motel had looked closer to Winsted than it turned out to be, so I decided to put off having dinner and plod on, despite the fact that the blister on my right foot had declared itself at last.

Then the rain started again, just as it got dark. My flashlight gave out. The commuter traffic from Hartford roared past, its headlights bouncing off the fluorescent ribbons on my staff. Tired, wet, and dismayed at having to brave the traffic in the night rain, I thought of the squashed squirrels, birds, chipmunks, frogs, skunks, snakes and raccoons I'd passed who'd come to grief crossing the road without a flashlight or even a few bright ribbons to ward off the enemy.

We're born pedestrians, but are everywhere trapped in cars. Walkers who cover great distances are struck by how monstrously a single means of transportation dominates even the most bucolic landscape, making it more dangerous, dirty and ugly than we admit.

How could we? Everyone drives—and for awhile that evening even I yearned to put the pedal to the metal.

Arrived after nine at my motel, in the middle of nowhere but next to a deserted shopping center and across from Satan's Kingdom State Park, where I learned from a brochure that runaway slaves, renegade Indians and outlaw whites had lived together in the eighteenth century. Despite the road aches in my legs and feet I was ravenous, so I hobbled next door to an Italian restaurant in the shopping center.

The young woman who ran the place was having a party with her friends, and the kitchen was closed, despite my entreaties. I ordered a drink, anyway, just to be around people. Then a couple left the party, a truck started up, and the building rocked. Quiet Connecticut had become Saigon. Everyone ran to the front. The departing couple had lobbed an M-80 firecracker in the door to say farewell.

Windsor Locks. Wednesday night. Passed through big, bustling Simsbury and quiet, tiny Tariffville on my way north to Windsor Locks, in the center of the state. Small villages on back roads all day. The sun was high, the air was cool, the countryside was lush, the foliage bright. To take my mind off my feet I kept an eye out for roadside souvenirs, finding a rubber snake and a pink cloth elephant among the beer bottles and fast-food boxes that littered the route.

A second blister—on my right foot—announced itself as I neared my bed for the night in a motel for Bradley International Airport. To get there I had to cross the gigantic parking lot of the Hamilton Watch Company, then cut across bleak open fields George Washington had complained of long before me. Jets roared overhead every ten minutes and rattled the windows of my motel, but I didn't care; I'd had dinner and my feet were elevated.

Stafford Springs. Thursday night. Limped slowly east on Route 190 all day after crossing the wide Connecticut River. Then it's shopping center after shopping center until at last I was out of the heavily populated middle of the state and back in the rolling countryside. It had been arranged that I'd stay in a private home because there are no public lodgings in Stafford Springs, even though it's a large mill town.

Once again I arrived late, and I hadn't eaten because there were no restaurants open. The son of the woman who agreed to put me up (she was off on vacation) answered my knock, commented, "You must have had quite a walk," and returned to his dinner. I watched television with his wife for a few minutes and then when he finished asked to see my bedroom. I was asleep by nine and up by first light and on my way to Woodstock.

The way to Woodstock is all uphill, along an old Indian path through pine forest. Deciduous trees were orange, their leaves half gone. I passed dairy farms where dozens of calves stood next to their individual sheds, and farm dogs that could hear a walker's soft footfall over the sounds of roaring trucks. At times there was more barking than birdsong. I was still dodging cars and cursing the arrogance of drivers. (Anti-DWI campaigns are fine, but what about the abuses of sober, normal drivers?)

I was due to arrive in Woodstock by noon, Friday, but by noon I had only reached a campground with a public phone five miles from the village, so I called Clarence Child, First Selectman of Woodstock, Connecticut. He wanted to walk with me into town, he said, and in ten minutes he was dropped off, a large man of forty-seven whose great-grandfather had also been First Selectman (the job is equivalent to our Town Supervisor) running under the slogan, "And a little child shall lead them."

Clarence admitted that he'd been worried about our keeping a conversation going for five miles, but after four days alone on the road I had plenty of chat in me. He liked to walk and hike, he said, but his town administrative duties kept him busy. We took short cuts on town roads to his village, passed often by trucks from his town highway department. Except for the lack of mountains the rolling countryside reminded me of home: stone walls, pine forest, mountain laurel.

We talked about how Woodstock, Connecticut was celebrating its Tercentenary. There had been an exhibition at which artifacts related to the local history of Industry, Communication, Natural History, Native Americans, Religion, Agriculture, and so forth were displayed. They'd produced a number of souvenirs, a handsome catalog of their exhibition, and had erected a number of historical markers. It had taken a committee of forty people and the support of the entire community over a three-year period to make their celebration such a success.

We were met on the road by Bill Barber, a retired postmaster with an avid interest in local history, by a photographer and two reporters, and by my companion, Sondra Howell, who had clocked the mileage I'd walked by following my route: I'd covered a zigzag 170.5 miles.

I'd found people in Connecticut reserved, because I was a stranger; but because we were Clarence Child's guests, we were no longer strangers. In Woodstock, people were warm and friendly. We were put up for the night on a dairy farm in a farm house built in 1820 and lived in continuously by the same family ever since. Our lively, charming hostess, Florence Young, is in her seventies, and quite willing to talk about her family, local history, or her museum quality collection of antiques, many of which were exhibited in the Tercentenary exhibition.

In the evening Clarence and his schoolteacher wife Barbara took us to Bald Hill, a fine local restaurant, where we sampled Woodstock wine from a local winery, and toasted the sister villages. After dinner Clarence and Barbara opened the Congregational Church, so we could see the results of recent interior renovation.

Saturday we attended a crafts fair at Roseland Cottage, on the large town green. Known locally as "the pink house," it is a Victorian gingerbread structure where presidents once came to stay, and speak.

We left Woodstock feeling like we were leaving Shangri-La, New England version, having been shown the most gracious hospitality. We brought home with us a lasting impression of a village not unlike own own, with a well developed pride in its long heritage. It's nice to walk up and down in the world and always find yourself back home in it.

# THE WOODSTOCK
# LAND CONSERVANCY:

## A Twentieth Anniversary
## Exploration

# Sloan Gorge Preserve

Will Nixon

IN ONE OF MY FAVORITE John Cheever stories, "The Swimmer," Neddy Merrill, the boyish but no-longer-young protagonist, decides, after finishing his glass of gin beside a friend's pool on a summer afternoon, to swim home via the backyard swimming pools strung across his suburban community. Inspired by this quixotic journey, I decided to mark the Woodstock Land Conservancy's twentieth anniversary by hiking across town on Conservancy lands. Though best known for the Zena Cornfield, the group owns six properties and protects nine others with conservation easements. Though we'd cheat a bit by car my friend Michael Perkins, a great walker and reader, was glad to join me.

I proposed that we start at the Sloan Gorge Preserve. "Never heard of it," said Michael, which didn't surprise me. This eighty-eight-acre forest parcel between West Saugerties Road and Stoll Road near the Woodstock/Saugerties town line has gone public rather quietly and gradually. On a sunny morning in mid-April we pulled into its small parking lot off Stoll Road. We had the place to ourselves.

The path led us through pines to the base of a bluestone quarry rubble pile, where a plaque honored Allan Edward Sloan, a Woodstock artist. "Never heard of him," said Michael, which did surprise me, since he loves local history. Allan Edward Sloan, as I later learned from his son Allan King Sloan of Lexington, Massachusetts, first came to Woodstock in the late 1920's while an art student at the National Academy of Design in New York City. After he married Charlotte King from Cleveland, his hometown, the couple moved their young family back and forth between Woodstock and Cleveland during the Depression, then settled into a home on Chestnut Hill Road after World War Two.

A portrait painter, Allan Edward Sloan worked the Christmas season at Saks Fifth Avenue, doing pastels of children. At home, though, his favorite subject was Overlook Mountain. Charlotte King wrote a weekly "What's Cookin?" column for the *Woodstock Townsman*. After her sudden death in 1970, he bought the eighty-eight-acre parcel with the notion that a relative from Cleveland might build a house on it. That never happened. Nor did he use the property himself. Impressed by the Conservancy's protection of the Zena Cornfield and other fields by his house on Chestnut Hill Road, Sloan left what he jokingly called "Snake Acres," his undeveloped land, to the group before dying in 1999. Both he and Charlotte King now lie among friends in the Woodstock Artists' Cemetery.

From 2004 to 2006, I served on the Conservancy board. By then, the group had decided to open this property to the public. (Step one: rename "Snake Acres" as "Sloan Gorge.") During the spring and summer of 2006, I made trips to the area as a member of a trail crew that nailed up yellow trail markers, cleared fallen branches, and chainsawed through fallen tree trunks to prepare the mile and a half loop that runs the length of the property. From the old quarry, an impressive rubble mound below the cliff walls that were mined, the trail leads into the gorge, which is modest as gorges go. I might call it a hemlock ravine, but even ravine sounds too dramatic. The streambed, which alternates between leaf-filled shallow pools and damp silty ground, passes through bedrock sides perhaps twenty feet high. The Grand Canyon it's not. Yet each time I've taken this trail I've slipped into that childhood imagination that sees things as larger than they are. The gorge becomes a miniature model of a towering canyon in Dinosaurland.

My favorite visit came the afternoon that Catskills geologist Bob Titus walked through Sloan Gorge for the first time. A ponytailed professor in a weathered green hat, he rushed up to cliffs then stood back at various angles like an art critic apprizing an exhibit much better than what he'd expected. Where I'd settled for childhood fantasies, he uncovered clues to an epic geological history. Some three hundred and seventy-five million years ago, he told us, the Catskills were equivalent to the Ganges Delta of today, the outwash from mountains that once towered like the Himalayas along the eastern horizon but had now worn down to the Berkshires. The bluestone layers of the Catskills were ancient river beds. The smile-like curve in one cliff's otherwise flat striation lines, he said, revealed the scouring created by a major flood. Within minutes he turned my understanding of the Catskills upside down. What I thought were mountains are, in fact, mud flats packed solid and thrust upwards by three hundred and seventy-five million years of plate tectonics. Alas, this knowledge hasn't made them any easier to climb.

Today, Sloan Gorge has geology trail markers along with an informative flier by Titus. The gorge wasn't carved by the piddling stream we see, but by white-water currents roaring down from melting Ice Age glaciers. In the past Sloan Gorge offered high drama. But Michael and I were content with the quiet retreat it now provides. "Not even a chain saw," he observed.

The gorge has several levels, though the ascents are so gentle that it's easy to miss the changes. In the middle section the trail hugs the cliff to remain above swampy pools black with leaf muck and green with moss. (I've learned the hard way not to walk through here at peak mosquito season in June.) As we clambered up and down alongside the cliff, we peered into crevices and stood under overhangs. "Shelter from the storm," Michael said. Under one protected corner I made an unusual find, a bed of porcupine scat laid out like small chocolate Easter eggs. I knelt to peek into the tiny cave mouth at the bottom of the stone alcove where the creature must hole up in the winter. Standing again, I found in front of my face a mossy bird's nest packed into a small cliff pocket like a woven throne.

By now Michael was enchanted. "This would be a nice place to camp," he said, staring out among the hemlocks. He's of an older Woodstock generation that once went skinny-dipping in Cooper Lake, so who's to say he wouldn't sneak into Sloan Gorge for a night? But, like me, he'd noticed that the spring awakening we'd been waiting for hadn't arrived. The bare trees fingering at the blue sky hadn't yet burst with tiny flowers at their tips. The few birds in the hemlocks had fallen silent. The brown leaf mat on the forest floor revealed no delicate wildflowers. The day was warm. But late winter still blanketed the land.

Then I heard a subtle but distinctive crackling noise. Ahead of me, Michael had walked right through it, so I called him back. The black shadows I saw at first glance on the leaf mat weren't shadows at all, but swarms of insects as tiny as pencil lead shavings. Thousands upon thousands upon thousands. Crawling, springing, massing—a living oil spill that stained leaves and rocks for several feet around. I'd never seen anything like it. If the new life of spring was what I wanted, here it was as a microscopic locusts' plague.

"Have you seen *Them*?" Michael asked. It was a 1950's science fiction film about giant ants created by the radiation released by atomic bomb tests in the New Mexico desert. The crackling noise on the leaves sounded like those mutant ants, if the volume could be cranked up a thousandfold.

"Is it any good?" I asked.

"One of the camp classics," Michael said. A cautionary tale of scientific hubris threatening to destroy us. A story that never goes out of style.

The secret revealed in "The Swimmer" is that the enthusiastic hero has gone mad. Neddy Merrill may think that he's passing through an enchanted land of bright sunshine, blossoming apple trees, and welcoming poolside laughter, but we realize by the end that he has lost his house and his family, and has fallen into a terrible delusion. But Michael and I weren't nuts. We were having fun discovering the wonders of nature no matter what they might be. Plus, we were just getting started. We had the rest of Woodstock to cross.

Sloan Gorge Preserve has a parking lot with a trail kiosk. Driving north from Woodstock on West Saugerties Road, veer right onto Goat Hill Road for another quick right, followed by a quick left onto Stoll Road. In a quarter mile or so, the parking lot will appear on the left. The website woodstocklandconservancy.org has more information. –W.N.

# Mount Guardian

Michael Perkins

IT WAS THE WEEK of the big Minnewaska fire, and although it was a cool sunny morning when Will Nixon and I climbed the westernmost hump of Mount Guardian, the smoke had cast a haze over the Hudson Valley.

It's an easy hike, much more so than the path up from Byrdcliffe I've climbed so many times. Just take MacDaniel Road to Mount Guardian Road and keep climbing. You'll come to an old logging trail. Park on the shoulder, and walk right up to heaven—which in this case is owned by the Woodstock Land Conservancy. (They acquired a parcel of eighteen acres at the ridgeline in 2000, nineteen acres in 2003, and twelve more in 2005.)

Will led the way, the summit being one of his favorite Woodstock places. After a forty-five-minute stroll we arrived at a boulder he jumped on. Below us the valley shimmered in the gentle sunlight, the ribbon of the Hudson far off to our left, and beyond it what Will guessed was the Fisher Center for the Performing Arts at Bard College designed by Frank Gehry. Its silvery roof signaled the words "Edifice Complex."

A fire ring by the boulder held a lone beer can. "There's a graffito up here," Will called. "1817." I tried to imagine what the view would have been like almost two centuries ago. All I could do was think of Chief Joseph Brant, the great Iroquois leader, looking down on a much smaller Woodstock hamlet during the Revolutionary War. Brant's Iroquois sided with the British, and Brant's forces had roamed the Catskills.

"Natural history's fine," I said. "But what humans have done on and to the landscape is equally important." I told him the story of Joseph Brant. We walked to another view, this time looking out over Cooper Lake and Ticeteneyck Mountain. The low green Catskills rippled away from us.

"You can really see where the mountains begin in Woodstock," Will commented, as we leaned back on our elbows like emperors surveying the works of the flatlanders below. Logging had changed the Catskills, we agreed, talking of the spots of first-growth timber to be found here and there in inaccessible hiding places. The area's first families had cut everything that could be gotten to, stopping only when a mountaintop would cost more to cut than it could be sold for. Something like the peak oil crisis we're faced with today, I thought idly, wondering if in ten years a new wave of logging—this time cutting trees for fuel—would sweep over the landscape we loved.

One of the unsung glories of hiking, if you're with a like-minded companion, is that a little exercise and a change of perspective makes for expansiveness. Easy speculation leads to the kind of philosophizing that might seem entirely too airy indoors. We spoke of everything from poetry to presidential politics, with only a pileated woodpecker's hammering to remind us, as we walked on dry leaves, that it it was quiet on the mountain. It's generally true that you have to climb above 2,000 feet—3,000 to be safe—before you can find genuine quiet in the Catskills, and even then the chain saw's diabolic whine rises to your ears.

It had not occurred to me before this hike, out of the hundreds I've gone on, that good talk *and* quiet might be inducements to get people out of their cars and away from their entertainment centers and onto the trail.

And that's what has kept me hiking: the higher you climb, the more perspective you gain on your life, and the more perspective you gain, the less seriously you take yourself. The more fun you have, the more you have to give to others.

Or that's how it works with me—you see what I mean about the mountain air making one expansive, perhaps even light-headed? But Will is a patient interlocutor, with a benign mien, so I rambled on as we descended Mount Guardian's western shoulder. It had been a perfect morning, so we only smiled when we got to Will's car and were blasted with rock music from a nearby house. Stifling the urge to run back up the mountain, we drove down into Woodstock, talking of our next adventure: Snake Rocks.

# Snake Rocks, Home of Oscar

Will Nixon

TO GIVE OUR LITTLE ADVENTURE literary pretensions, I'd chosen Neddy Merrill, the protagonist of John Cheever's short story "The Swimmer," to inspire our tour celebrating the Woodstock Land Conservancy's twentieth anniversary. But when Michael and I climbed onto Snake Rocks, an old bluestone quarry, I could see that my clever analogy between life and literature was breaking down. Neddy Merrill rushed from pool to pool, "the Grahams, the Hammers, the Lears, the Howlands, and Crosscups." Then "the Bunkers," "the Levys," "the Hallorans, the Saches, the Biswangers, Shirley Adams, the Gilmartins, and the Clydes." Our guide swam through the social register. Yet the pools sounded the same.

At Snake Rocks I marveled at the differences among the Conservancy's properties. We'd started at Sloan Gorge Preserve, a hemlock ravine carved by waters roaring down from Ice Age glaciers, but now an intermittent stream, offering us geology lessons and a serene escape from our morning chores.

Then we'd climbed the western hump of Mount Guardian to my favorite lookout with its panoramic view of Cooper Lake and the western Woodstock mountains. Seated on this kingly stone outcropping, Michael had told me about Chief Joseph Brant of the Iroquois, who'd shared leadership over this land with Woodstock villagers at the time of the American Revolution.

Now, having climbed atop this massive slope of loose rocks to explore the quarry pools tucked below the back cliffs, our imaginations ran in new directions. On the eastern wing of this extensive rubble heap we discovered a bluestone sculpture studio. Someone, or several people, had stacked rocks in cairns, benches, and sundial-like pedestals with a lone slab angled off the top.

After a dozen sculptures Michael stopped counting. "Everywhere you look, you see another one," he said, impressed by both the work and the whimsy invested in these pieces. "As much as I believe in wilderness," he added, "it's the human that I look for in landscapes." At Snake Rocks we'd come to the right place.

Under a misty overcast—Michael used his umbrella for a walking stick—spring was bursting. Small white birches rooted amid the rocks wore mustard green tassels. The pin cherry trees held their last white flower petals amid their first leaves. An oak shrub unfurling leaves stained nutmeg purple stopped me in my tracks. Spring's colors, though subtle, delighted me as much as autumn's.

Add the pine trees, the moss, and the cattails in a pool, and Snake Rocks had the atmosphere of a meditative garden. Then I heard my first black-throated green warbler of the year, *zee zee zee zoo zee*, a five-syllable song I'd once used in a haiku. Art was in the air.

In the center of a natural amphitheater Michael stood on a smooth slab for a stage and faced the rock rubble slope that would provide natural seating for the poetry reading he'd started planning. "We'll put ten people there," he said, then turned around to stare up at the smooth cliffs rising twenty feet to a rim of white pines: the balcony. Imagining myself reading to a cliff top audience, I had the same reaction Michael did. "This could be intimidating," he admitted. "You'd want to be on your best game."

Of course, no one had planned for Snake Rocks to be so enchanting. With his sense of history Michael saw more here than sculpture mounds and poetry readings. "I think of all the poor bastards who carried the bluestone out," he said, referring to the quarrymen paid almost nothing for their labor. For years, the Woodstock Guild gift shop sold an old photo postcard of the Snake Rocks quarry active in the early 1900's. Surely, those men didn't foresee the day when their dangerous work site would become a nature sanctuary where a pair of poets could clamber about the waste rock piles satisfying their aesthetic spirits. But here we were. By now I'd decided Snake Rocks should be a Chinese Poetry Garden.

In 1960 or so, the town of Woodstock resurveyed all its lands and discovered that no one owned the thirty-six acres of this old quarry on the ridgeline above the Wittenberg Sportsmen's Club valley. J.C. Van Rijn, the founder of Rotron and a founder of the town planning board, learned of this unclaimed parcel and bought it for less than $1,000. In 1962, he gave it to his daughter, Eva Van Rijn, who planned to build a house, until she and her husband, Ed Chavez, learned that they didn't have a right of way on the quarry road. Rather than fighting the neighbor in court, they let the matter lay.

In 2004, more than a decade after her husband died, Van Rijn and her current partner gave the property to the Woodstock Land Conservancy. A longstanding supporter of the Nature Conservancy as well, she viewed this donation as "the only thing I could do. If I was a multimillionaire, I'd buy land for bike paths all around Woodstock." But she's not. She's a painter, particularly of Western landscapes, who still walks at Snake Rocks every week except in winter. She appreciates the way Conservancy has left the place the way it was. "They've respected it very much."

Michael and I scrambled down from the sculpture wing of the expansive rubble pile to visit my favorite hideaway in Snake Rocks, a quarry pool almost like a swimming pool with its far end squared-off by the former digging. I loved studying its dark waters until I spotted the first lazy flashes of the goldfish that added the perfect Chinese touch.

"That's my fault," Eva Van Rijn sheepishly admitted, when we spoke by phone. She knows goldfish aren't native to Catskill quarry ponds. But years ago, when she had to remove goldfish from her yard pond, she couldn't bear to kill them. So she brought them to Snake Rocks to "give them the rest of the summer." Little did she know they'd survive under the winter ice and breed for years to come.

She wasn't the only one. She once met a couple releasing their beloved pet, Oscar, an orange and white fantail goldfish, into the pool. Moving from the area, they couldn't bring Oscar, too, so they set him loose among friends at Snake Rocks. Van Rijn hasn't seen Oscar in a while, but who's to say his offspring aren't with us still?

Perhaps the classic Chinese poet Li Po had Oscar in mind when he wrote:

Why talk of cleansing elixirs of immortality?
Here, the world's dust rinsed from my face,

I'll stay close to what I've always loved,
content to leave that peopled world forever.

# The Stories Landscapes Tell

Michael Perkins

FOLLOWING OUR PLAN of exploring Woodstock Land Conservancy holdings, Will Nixon and I went to the Zena Cornfield, but the morning was overcast, the hay was knee high, and the ticks were thick. On a clear day, the twenty-two-acre cornfield, acquired by the Conservancy in 1989, offers the best view of Woodstock's mother mountain range. The field has been cultivated for hundreds of years. As Zena is the oldest part of Woodstock, this great open space is one of the symbolic centers of our town. It's not highly touted, it's not spectacularly grand; there are other sites in Ulster County with more scenic pizazz. But if you don't feel something like awe as you drive past it, if instead you wonder why such a large parcel hasn't been developed, then you probably enjoyed seeing the large picture frame that was put there awhile back. The empty frame claimed the view, while announcing that Kilroy had been there.

Pressing on, we drove up Chestnut Hill Road to another Conservancy property, Ludins Field, a six-acre hayfield with nothing remarkable about it—except that it is open land, and open land, without picture frames is what makes the difference between country and suburbs. Once again, it didn't seem worth walking because of the minuscule blood-suckers lying in wait. So I suggested we take a look at Yankeetown Pond, which Will had not seen except from Snake Rocks.

I've been stopping on long bicycle rides and walks at Yankeetown Pond for over thirty years, but I knew very little about it, other than that it was a lovely pit stop. Just take the Wittenberg Road from Bearsville, make a left at the intersection with the Glenford-Wittenberg Road (the old Ulster & Delaware Turnpike) and a mile later make a left onto Pond Road and park.

Gaze out over the pond's expanse, as I did one summer long ago:

July brings an armada
to Yankeetown Pond. Lilies set forth
on flat green boats.

Will and I walked to the edge, looking for a path around the pond. A large snapping turtle sat on a rock, ignoring us. An owl hooted. Logs in the feeder stream indicated that beaver engineers had been hard at work. We walked into the woods, looking for a path around the pond, but found only a road marked private, so we emerged and walked up Pond Road to its cul-de-sac dead end, and walked back to the car feeling somewhat frustrated. Our only remaining strategy was serendipity.

I was sitting in Will's car with the door open, gazing out over the pond and wishing I knew more about its mysteries, when a friendly spirit materialized next to me. This *genius loci*, yclept, as I learned, Steve Morris, had a long white pony tail and leaned on a long, stout walking staff. Steve lives near the pond, and was a ready font of information. Will, who had been watering a bush, returned, and the three of us talked.

I asked about the geese I'd often come across at the pond, and Steve said there was still a family that came to visit and feed on the bass and perch. Steve builds boats, and recalled the days when he'd launch them right where we stood. I remembered that there had been sawmills at Yankeetown, and from Steve and other sources I pieced together a history, from mills to kayaks.

Retreating ice sheets left boulders, gravel, and clay that formed natural dams making the pond possible. Zachary and Peter Short, Jr. were the area's first settlers. Other settlers gathered around the sawmill set up at the outlet of Yankeetown during the 1790's. Later, Daniel Lumberd and John Eldridge leased acreage on the Little Beaverkill just below the stream's source in Yankeetown Pond and built their sawmill, which stood on the new Ulster & Delaware Turnpike, enabling them to send lumber to Kingston and points west.

The history of sawmills at the pond reaches into the 1940's and 1950's, when Tom Shultis operated a mill there powered by a water turbine.

We asked Steve who owned Yankeetown Pond. A loosely formed neighborhood association owns a piece of it, as does the

Wittenberg Sportsmen's Club. New York City owns six hundred acres, and the best access to hiking around Yankeetown Pond is via their property up at Snake Rocks. Private landowners hold the rest. In the old days, squatters occupied the valley below Snake Rocks and were called "Vly (for valley) Yonders."

The pond has some romantically spooky aspects to it. Steve said that many of the grassy hummocks that look like islands in the middle of the pond are not: if you set foot on them you would sink into a bog.

Yankeetown Pond has a ghost named Sebastian Rhinehart, who came home from the Civil War and lived on an island in the pond in a dugout shelter. His wife didn't want to live underground like a marsupial, so she left him for another man. The story has it that Sebastian Rhinehart murdered their daughter, although he was never charged with the crime, and his bones lie on one of those untrustworthy islands.

Steve strolled off down the Ulster & Delaware Turnpike, and I found myself thinking about the stories landscapes have to tell. For three decades I have been visiting the pond and had never heard its story. Then because of the adventitious arrival of a tutelary spirit in the form of Mr. Morris, the pond began to call out to me. Although we had not found a path, Will and I did not repine, for we had heard the pond.

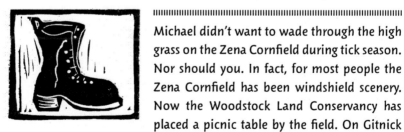

IIIIIIIIIIIIIIIIIIIIIIIIIIIIIIIIIIIIIIIIIIIIIIIIIIIIIIIIIIIIIIIIIIIIIIIIIIIIIIIIIIIIIIIII
Michael didn't want to wade through the high grass on the Zena Cornfield during tick season. Nor should you. In fact, for most people the Zena Cornfield has been windshield scenery. Now the Woodstock Land Conservancy has placed a picnic table by the field. On Gitnick Road just off Route 212 the spot has a tremendous view of the field and Overlook Mountain. –W.N.
IIIIIIIIIIIIIIIIIIIIIIIIIIIIIIIIIIIIIIIIIIIIIIIIIIIIIIIIIIIIIIIIIIIIIIIIIIIIIIIIIIIIIIIIIIIIIIIIII

# A Five-Minute Walk Up Into Splendor

Will Nixon

FOR SOME REASON, I like walking in the woods not only to escape society's conflicts but to find them as well. It's the journalist in me. After Bush won the 2000 election, I visited the Arctic National Wildlife Refuge that he wanted to drill. Before GE agreed to dredge PCBs in the Upper Hudson, I explored their dump sites on the riverbanks, green meadows planted on black landfill tarps. Swallows nesting nearby laid eggs that qualified as hazardous waste. Fortunately, Woodstock has avoided that kind of disaster, though you wouldn't know it from the rhetoric in our public debates.

For our final walk celebrating the Woodstock Land Conservancy's twentieth anniversary, Michael Perkins and I started at California Quarry, eager to see Woodstock's first cell tower pine tree, *Pinus cellula controversia*. The Open Space Institute's purchase of almost two hundred acres of quarry land from the Town of Woodstock is their biggest step yet in an effort with the Conservancy to more than double the size of the Overlook Wild Forest within the state's Catskill Forest Preserve. Anyone who thinks that Overlook has enough houses perched on its flanks will be sympathetic to this campaign to protect the slopes that remain wild.

As we entered the quarry property, I thought of Snake Rocks, a smaller quarry owned by the Conservancy. Blessed with nooks and crannies, low cliffs, small pools, and bluestone sculptures, Snake Rocks had the charm of a rock garden featuring birch trees, moss carpets, and a magical goldfish pond. In stark contrast, California Quarry has the weedy grimness of an old gravel mine. The massive embankments offer little but dirt slides and rock slabs and scattered greens shrubs knotted into the steep soil. The gravel clearing appears worn with tire tracks and dried puddles. Beyond the clearing, there's a fenced-in plot of sumac bushes, the site of several previous transmission towers. There's also a grove of dead weathered trees. Branches claw toward the sun as if beseeching a god that failed them.

Entering the woods, though, we quickly came to a road that ramps up to the top of the embankment for one of Woodstock's unpublicized treasures: a panoramic view of Woodstock and the Hudson Valley unlike any other. "Oh yeah," said Michael, who hadn't been here before. "This is marvelous."

While the Overlook summit view is justly famous—on clear days you can see the Berkshires by facing one way; High Point, New Jersey, by facing the other—the view from the embankment is more intimate. It's like looking out an airplane moments after takeoff when the landscape remains close and buildings are toy-sized, but suddenly you can see the horizon. This morning, Michael and I looked out upon the Shawangunk Ridge with its sharp hump above Mohonk, the eastern end of the Ashokan reservoir, and Ohayo Mountain standing at our height. The valley between was a choppy ocean of dark summer trees. A solitary white steeple marked the village of Woodstock. The illusion of an unbroken wilderness was much stronger than from higher up the mountain. "You wouldn't believe there are enough people out there to need cell phones," said Michael. We could have been looking back three hundred years to the age of smoke signals.

California Quarry had a colorful history in the nineteenth century. Supposedly named after California gold rush fever, it was the largest of many quarries on the lower slopes of Overlook worked by immigrants who lived in Irish Village in Lewis Hollow. "These lively, often boisterous people lived intensely, danced on a wooden platform in the woods, drank heavily at their shebeens and produced their large families," wrote Alf Evers in *Woodstock: History of an American Town*. On election day they got drunk and brawled with the locals on the Village Green.

Bluestone quarrying was a boom and bust business that shifted by the 1840's from serving local needs, such as chimney stones, basement flooring, and gravestones, to supplying New York City with sidewalks. Not until the 1920's did it finally die out, replaced by cement. The rest of the twentieth century proved rather tame, save for a "No Camping" ordinance passed by the town board in 1969 to prevent hippies from taking over the quarry. In 1949, Eleanor Cannon, a wealthy Woodstock bohemian originally from Chicago, and her husband Victor deeded the quarry to the town for $1. Another $1 deed in 1964 had expanded the town holdings to almost two hundred acres, much of it on the steep hillside above the quarry.

In February 2006 the town board under Supervisor Jeremy Wilber unanimously voted to sell one hundred and eight-six acres of this property to OSI for $186,600. The town would have kept twelve acres for the cell tower. When Jeff Moran became Supervisor, he reworked the deal in a small but significant way. It turns out that the town highway department still uses the quarry as a quarry on occasion. When Mink Hollow flooded in the spring of 2006, town crews worked through the night under lights in California Quarry to load dump trucks with embankment material to repair Mink Hollow Road so that residents wouldn't be trapped. Rather than selling these embankments, as initially planned, the town has kept them and will instead lease the gravel clearing to the state Department of Environmental Conservation to provide a public parking lot.

Nor did Moran want to give up the cliff top with its panoramic vista. "It's a five-minute walk up into splendor," he says of one of his favorite mountain views in the country. Under his plan Woodstock rather that the Catskill Forest Preserve will own this vista, but the purpose will the same, the creation of a public park in what has been a semi-forbidden and forgotten mining site. (Michael and I passed a "No Trespassing" sign to get there, apparently a common practice.)

Yet we'd also come to see the cell tower. From a distance, walking Plochmann Lane, I'd decided that it resembled a green pipe cleaner, an oddity but hardly as ugly as such towers can be along highways where they're rocket-sized toilet brushes. Up close, though, our cell pine proved to be impressive. Its brown metal trunk was worthy of a sequoia. Its branches screwed into the trunk didn't start until the canopy height of the surrounding forest. While natural trees stood independently, living off nothing more than roots and sunshine, this one has a fenced-in support compound with electrical equipment boxes and a windowless tan building that hummed and clicked like an industrial refrigerator. Several dozen black cables were inserted into its trunk for electrical IV. Green plastic garlands hid the tower's tricornered transmission arms. Birds from neighboring trees didn't dare fly up into its heights.

I had to admit, the damned thing was an impressive pillar of science. Craning my neck to look up the top, I thought of the Washington Monument. Not Michael. "It's an artificial Christmas tree for the poison gifts of our civilization," he announced. Needless to say, he didn't have a cell phone. Minutes earlier, he'd conceded that if we're going to build cell towers we should disguise them. Now he was sharpening his wit for our climb up California Quarry Road. A few years earlier, when I served on the Conservancy board, I'd become obsessed with this road. It fed my fantasies of becoming a land savior. Then it broke my heart. Now I wanted to hear what Michael had to say.

# Mount Hubris

Will Nixon

AFTER VISITING Woodstock's cell tower pine in California Quarry Michael Perkins and I began our climb up California Quarry Road. Everyone in Woodstock knows this road, whether they realize it or not. Whenever you look up at the handful of houses perched on Overlook's steep slopes like alien invaders from the canyons of L.A., you're admiring, or more likely resenting, homes served by this road. In the Catskills, which has a remarkable history of protecting scenic mountainsides, these houses stand out as the garish exceptions. The white one in the middle could be Woodstock's unofficial lighthouse the way it shines so boldly in sunshine.

Yet how many people have hiked up this road? Not Michael. Though an inveterate walker, he'd always taken the pretty route, Meads Mountain Road, when ascending from the village to the Overlook summit. Now we came to the first steep curve that banks up and around like a roller coaster ride. "This is a hell of a hill," said Michael, leaning into his walking stick. I concurred. Never have I walked this road without vowing—and panting—to get more exercise. To me this route is the toughest road walk in town.

The next curve widens like a cul-de-sac in the hemlocks. The town road ends and the private road starts, an obvious change-over to old pavement that's pitted and cracked. We paced ourselves up this long straightaway, passing a side road called Rock Ledge and leaving behind the settled, historic village of Woodstock that has discretely spread up into the valleys. Finally, this relentless pitch reached a sharp bend over a culvert pipe hiding a mountainside gully. Here the crumbling pavement ends. The true drama begins.

An impressive dirt road has plowed, blasted, and filled its way over ridgelines and up across a mountainside bowl. There's nothing settled or historic about it. Water rivulets keep eroding the dirt road. Dump trucks occasionally inch upwards to pour fresh layers of soil. The fresh phone poles near the top don't yet have wires. From here on up, California Quarry Road serves the brash outpost of high-elevation houses that have conquered their way up the mountain.

In 1952, Eleanor Cannon, a wealthy Woodstocker originally from Chicago, who'd already deeded the quarry itself to the town, sold three hundred acres to her neighbor, William E. West, whose family gradually developed the California Quarry Road we have today. Back then, the pavement ended a few hundred feet past the turnoff to Chimney Road, now near the bottom, while an old haul road continued up to the quarry. From 1968 to 1976 the Wests built the road to the top, as Don West, one of William E. West's sons, later told me by phone. Some twenty-five houses now use the road, many of them hidden off in the woods on the lower reaches. The handful up high, those visible from town, went up in the 1980's and 1990's.

On my first climb years ago I met a dog walker coming down who told me the road continued up to a bulldozer parked at the top. I didn't find the bulldozer, but at the final zigzag ramp blasted in the slope, I did find the rock rubble of a roadbed under construction. The destruction was awful. Yet the view was spectacular, a panorama of the Catskills I'd expect to find an hour up a trail, not in someone's future driveway. So began my love/hate relationship with California Quarry Road. I deeply disliked the sight of these mountainside houses and their road scars. Yet if I had more money and less scruples, I would have bought one in a minute.

On a misty day several years ago, churning with such thoughts while returning down the road, I happened to look up at a plywood house being built on a prominent outcropping. For weeks, I'd seen this house from the valley, a blond billboard as tacky as the Hollywood Hills. But up close in the mist it was a plywood castle. If Woodstock had a Great Gatsby, I decided, he'd live on California Quarry Road. On my next walk I'd entered the unfinished living room to admire the picture-window view of Ashokan High Point and other mountains I knew. What would it be like to live with such grandeur all the time, rather than having to march up to a summit for a twenty-minute fix every week or two?

Marching up a steep curve, Michael and I found ourselves by this house, now finished. Happily, it's painted forest green and has a screened-in porch giving it the feeling of a camp cottage rather than a nouveau riche trophy home. I told Michael my Gatsby tale anyway. He took to it immediately.

"Old Money would never do this," he said. "They would think it vulgar to live up here." Indeed, the divide between the rich and the rest of society is starkly displayed on the upper reaches of this road in a way not seen elsewhere in Woodstock where the celebrated and the wealthy live privately removed. Up here, the houses lord over the valley. Everyone can see them. But few people reach them. A masseuse once told me that when her car tires began spinning out on the dirt incline she parked and wheeled her massage table the rest of the way up to her client's house. What better image of servants and masters do we need?

"I feel a song coming on," Michael said with a sly grin.

I've got that Gatsby feeling,
Made my money lying and stealing...

The rest of his tune doesn't belong in a family publication.

The final curve was the steepest yet. Looking back across the mountainside bowl we saw a fresh brown gouge in the forested hillside, where the yellow arm of a Caterpillar claw was digging a new house platform. The grinding and scraping that echoed across the valley provided the appropriate soundtrack for the end of our climb. By now we could see the Hudson Highlands along the southern horizon. Michael sat down on the guardrail for a water break. He'd lost his enthusiasm. "I've climbed lots of mountains," he said. "This is the worst." Plodding up the dirt reminded him of watching Erich von Stroheim's silent film, *Greed*, which has scenes of a man walking across Death Valley. "It's a classic," Michael said of the movie. "But it's boring. And it's endless."

The water revived him. "This is Mount Hubris," he announced.

Above the topmost house we came to a side drive that hooks around the ridgeline away from Woodstock to an overlook facing Saugerties and the Hudson. This was where I'd fantasized about saving one special spot from the bulldozers. This was where I'd gotten my heart broken over land conservation.

When I joined the Conservancy board, the group had its sights on this property. After hearing about it at meetings, I hiked up California Quarry Road for the first time and fell in love instantly. This spot has the best view of them all—not of Woodstock, but of the Hudson River Valley to the Taconic hills of Connecticut. When the oaks are bare, it looks across the upper slopes of Lewis Hollow to the summit fire tower. This amazing vista is also the problem. A house here would be the most visible yet on the road, the first seen from the fire tower. This small clearing has a raised gravel bed that struck me as the ideal platform for a lean-to, not somebody's Shangri-La country house.

As part of the Overlook Campaign, the Open Space Institute had a plan to buy this property. Though a bystander, I eagerly followed developments at meetings. Each time I stood in this clearing for the views, I renewed my enthusiasm for serving on the board. One day I'd be able to say I helped save this place. Once, noticing the real estate sign toppled in the weeds by the drive entrance, I considered sneaking it home under my jacket as a souvenir.

Then someone else bought the property. I was stunned. How could someone spoil my dream? Yet what had I done but sit through meetings, hike up for views, and fancy that I was saving this place by the force of my good intentions? The property belonged to the man who paid for it, not to my vanities as a land conservationist.

Yet I couldn't let go. I daydreamed about striking it rich with a screenplay to buy the property myself. (That happy delusion carried me up the road one blissful afternoon.) Or I'd meet a gazil-lionaire conservationist. (Instead, I met a low bidder on the prop-erty who'd driven up to visit the parcel on a winter afternoon, perhaps feeling wistful, though he was happy with his new house on Goat Hill Road.)

Not until a few summers after I'd left the board did fate inter-vene, when I directed a visiting land-use planner from the Adiron-dack Mountain Club up to the site. He drove us in his small station wagon and admired the views, but I suspect that he wondered what I expected him to do about the situation. Descending, he shifted into low gear, but near the bottom pulled off the road, as black smoke wafted up from his hood. He'd burned out his brakes. I finally had to accept that I wasn't going to save my three acres on Overlook Mountain, no matter how sacred they seemed to me.

"You can see forever, all right," said Michael, as we walked out onto the raised gravel platform. But he was more impressed by the fact, which I shared with him, that this platform was a septic system installed years ago to attract a future home builder. "The perfect metaphor," he decided. "You climb Mount Hubris to stand on a pile of shit."

I had to smile. His Mount Hubris was the dirt road gashing its way up to houses perched where houses didn't belong. Mine had been my fantasy of stopping it simply by sitting through meet-ings and climbing up for the views. Michael made me chuckle at my foolishness.

We started down the steep road. Michael planted his walking stick to avoid slipping on the loose dirt. He told me of Gatsby-like characters who'd moved to Woodstock in the past. "They wanted to buy their way into Woodstock Society, as if there is such a thing," he said. I listened attentively, for Michael tells wonderful stories about this town he's lived in for decades. But I knew there was a different story behind us, farther up the mountain than we'd climbed.

One spring day I hadn't stopped at the top of California Quarry Road, but had kept scrambling up through the bare forest on loose leaves and wobbly rocks, often barging through mountain laurels. In twenty minutes I reached the top of the climb, the rounded pyramid peak above all the houses seen from the village. I sat on a boulder and anointed myself king. Here my castle would rule over Woodstock. Yet, even better, I knew such a thing would never happen, for I sat in the middle of a seventy-five-acre property that OSI had acquired from the KTD monastery in 2005.

Years earlier, a couple had bought this land from Don West with the intention of building their dream house, but they'd later given it to KTD with the suggestion that the monastery construct retreat cabins on this wild ridgetop about a mile as the crow flies from their compound on Meads Mountain Road. "We didn't feel that was appropriate," Patrick Cliett, the KTD building manager, later told me by phone. The monastery wanted the land to be preserved. The Overlook Campaign gave them the buyer they wanted. In fact, KTD turned down a $500,000 offer from builders in order to sell the property to OSI for $387,000.

At the time KTD was embroiled in controversy over its expansion plans at Meads Mountain Road, so it didn't get much credit for insuring that these seventy-five acres of wild forest will forever remain King of the Mountain. So let me now thank KTD. And OSI. And the Woodstock Land Conservancy for enabling Michael and me to spend a season exploring its marvelous properties spread about town. We look forward to discovering the natural gems the Conservancy protects in its next twenty years.

# LOST ROADS

# The Low Peaks Fantasy Trail

Will Nixon

FOR TEN YEARS, I drove past Mount Tobias without quite knowing
what it was. Sure, I saw it from Route 212 in Willow, that mountain south of the meadow, or while passing Cooper Lake, the hump
beyond the water, but if you'd pressed me, I would have hesitated
and said, "I think that's Mount Tobias." I certainly didn't know
it in my heart, not the way I knew Overlook in Woodstock or
Mount Tremper in Phoenicia, two mountains with popular trails
and commanding fire tower views. On those summits you could
stake a claim to the green kingdom.

On my hiking map Mount Tobias had a green swatch of state
owned "Forever Wild" land, but no trails. Plus, it stood 2,550
feet tall, a pip-squeak among the Catskill High Peaks that reach
over 4,000 feet. Mount Tobias seemed so inconsequential that I
drove Wittenberg Road for a decade before realizing that the rolling up and downs were, in fact, the lower slopes of this mountain
all but hidden behind roadside trees save for glimpses up at its
ridgelines.

Then Michael DeWan turned my head around. On a spring
morning in 2006, Michael, then president of the Woodstock
Land Conservancy, led a group up to the Conservancy's property
on the western summit of Mount Guardian, which has an open
forest with a fire ring and a solitary boulder bearing an eroded
nineteenth century graffito. Continuing a hundred feet down
into the balsam fir forest we reached a cliff outcropping like a
castle turret above the trees on the steep hillside. The view was
magnificent, a panorama of western Woodstock as I hadn't seen
it before: Cooper Lake below, the wide Beaver Kill Valley in the
middle distance, an impressive ring of mountains surrounding it
all. This landscape was far more dramatic than I'd realized from
the car. And I'd hiked almost none of it.

I'll admit I'm a peak bagger. Within a year of moving to the Catskills in 1996, I'd climbed all thirty-five peaks over 3500 feet as listed by the Catskill 3500 Club. Then I'd climbed them several times over with friends earning their own club patches. Eventually, I turned into a bore, a been-there, done-that, know-it-all hiker. From the Mount Guardian lookout, though, I saw a Catskills I didn't know: the Low Peaks, I decided to call them. So what if they didn't rank high in elevation. They didn't need to. They rose from the low valley into true mountain profiles. On the map Mount Tobias might stand only 2,550 feet tall, but seen from Mount Guardian, it was massive, a broadly shouldered mountain that stretched the length of the Beaver Kill Valley. And it was one of half a dozen prominent peaks.

North of the valley, a steep nose ran up to the long flat ridgeline of Olderbark, a near-miss Catskill 3500 Club peak at 3,440 feet that I'd never bothered to bushwhack because I'd heard it was tough. (Indeed it was, I discovered a month later, though that long ridge offered thousands of yellow trout lilies flowering under the bright sun in the still winter bare forest.)

At the far end of the valley, I now saw, Mount Tremper was not one mountain but a trio of summits: Mount Tremper itself, a nameless one in the center, and Carl Mountain to the north. (Another nasty bushwhack, that Carl Mountain, I learned in July, especially for my friend Peter Koch who wore shorts only to wade repeatedly through stinging nettles. For the first time I heard Peter, the most ardent of environmentalists, invoke the F-word to describe plants.)

South of Mount Tobias, there stood Ticeteneyck Mountain, equally tall but more conical, rather alp-like compared to the flatter ridges common in the Catskills. Coming east, Ticeteneyck dipped sharply into a notch with its lower neighbor, Tonshi Mountain. I'd seen both from the Ashokan Reservoir on the other side, where they looked tamed by houses high up the slopes. From Mount Guardian they appeared wild. (Hera, the artist, later led a group of us up Ticeteneyck on woods roads that led to great reservoir lookouts. But when hiking with Hera, I learned, you saw her at the start and spent the rest of your time trying to catch up.)

Standing on the Mount Guardian outcropping, admiring the mountain topography of western Woodstock for the first time, I understood my friend Dave Holden's vision for a new trail—call it the Woodstock Trail—linking these Low Peaks.

Many Woodstockers have known Dave as a friendly counterman at Sunflower who keeps the last of his fine gray hair balled in a small ponytail. (If he trusted your indulgence, he'd treat you to puns.) Or they think of him as "Ranger Dave," the volunteer steward at the Comeau Property. I've had the good fortune to meet him as the mapper of Woodstock's lost roads. In his free time he dons moccasins, a vest with multiple pockets for notepads and maps, and his straw sun hat to venture into the woods to map the old roads that seem to run everywhere through our forests (except on bushwhacks, when I need them). Taking GPS measurements, he plots inch by inch with a red pen on enlarged contour maps the forgotten routes left by quarrymen, blueberry pickers, woodsmen, and travelers generations ago. To walk in the woods with Dave is to notice wagon ruts in the bedrock or trees with L-bent trunks that Native Americans grew as directional signals in the centuries before road signs.

These old roads provide a *de facto* hiking trail system. (Hera knows her roads on Ticeteneyck. I know mine in the woods between Sawkill Road and Route 28. No doubt, many Woodstockers know their own walking routes on woods roads that have no names and forgotten histories.) Perhaps this trail system might one day be legalized. (There is that pesky matter of "No Trespassing" signs.)

On a summer afternoon I brought Dave up to Mount Guardian to share the view. One of the Catskills' most famous trails is the Devil's Path, which roller coasters across the High Peaks of Indian Head, Twin, Sugarloaf, and Plateau Mountains. Thanks to connector trails, a hiker may start in the Overlook Mountain parking area and finish two or three days later on the summit of Mount Tremper after hiking the Devil's Path and more. Why not finish the loop? Dave asked.

A new trail down from Mount Tremper could cross Route 212 to climb Mount Tobias. From Tobias it could descend to Cooper Lake. After crossing Cooper Lake Hill, it could climb the steep western slopes of Mount Guardian to the lookout where Dave and I stood. Then it could continue across the three summits of Mount Guardian (another nasty bushwhack, but only in the mountain laurels at the eastern end) to finish at the parking lot for Overlook Mountain. Anyone who completed this loop would be leg weary and hungry for pizza after days of camping food, but also proud and impressed by Woodstock, a town not typically known for its hiking.

Considered from the Mount Guardian lookout, the Woodstock Trail seemed so obvious as to already exist. But the hard part of building this trail wouldn't be building the trail. It would be getting permission from landowners, a process both easier and harder than it might seem. Easier in that much of the land is owned by public entities. The upper reaches of Mount Tobias belong to the state Catskill Forest Preserve or the New York City Department of Environmental Protection, which has quietly become the largest landowner in western Woodstock in order to protect its Ashokan Reservoir watershed. The Woodstock Land Conservancy and the Town of Woodstock own important parcels on Mount Guardian. It's the private owners in between that might make this trail harder, if not impossible to create. After all, people have failed for years to get permission for a streamside path along the Sawkill from behind the Bearsville Theater to Rick Volz Field, a route of less than a mile. By this standard a Woodstock Trail over two major mountains and a hill would be a pipe dream.

Maybe it isn't a good idea. Come to think of it, forget I mentioned it. For as I stood with Dave on the Mount Guardian outcropping and marveled at the mountain panorama, I appreciated the fact that I had the Low Peaks to myself and my friends. (Trust me, on those bushwhacks we met nobody.)

Of these half a dozen mountains the one I returned to was Mount Tobias. Why? I wasn't sure. It didn't have views. It had a monstrous mountain laurel thicket on the south side. (Another nasty bushwhack, until Dave, who didn't share my tolerance for punishing bushwhacks, found old blueberry trails running through it.) Yet its charms kept calling me back. There was an open park-like forest filled with grass and ferns. Woods roads ran in many directions, waiting to be explored. (On one we found a rusty mailbox, a joke put up for a nearby hunter's cabin. Opening the rusty lid, we found a bird's nest for airmail.) On one outing I took a photo that I treasured of Dave seated with Michael Perkins on a log in the grassy forest on the summit. Dave wore on a tan vest, green shirt, and gray pants, while Michael had a blue shirt with its tails out and a rumpled white hat. His walking stick rested against his knee. They could have been the Hatfields or the McCoys, mountain men from a century ago who'd gone out to check their stills. (Michael is proud of his Kentucky family heritage). Yet they were sitting in Woodstock, a Woodstock that few people know.

Standing at the Mount Guardian lookout, Dave directed my eyes across the wide hump of Mount Tobias about halfway down from the summit toward Beetree Hill. He asked if I could make out the straight line in the trees that dropped down beyond Cooper Lake to cross toward Mink Hollow. That line was Whispell Road, he said. For hundreds of years, it had been an Indian path and then a farm road. It had last appeared on a map in 1898. But it was still there, Dave assured me. Still waiting to be hiked.

Here's a mystery: neither the USGS maps nor popular hiking maps show Abbey Road on Mount Tobias. But there is public access to state land near the top of Abbey Road, which is off Wittenberg Road. At the final turn before the turnaround at the top of Abbey Road, there's a gap in the stone wall on the uphill side. I park on Abbey Road and walk up. You may drive the dirt tracks between the wall to park above on the grass. You won't find marked trails. You will find woods roads to explore. –W.N.

# Whispell Road

Will Nixon

CALL US THE LOST ROADS GANG. Led by Dave Holden, who has spent countless hours mapping woods roads, we pulled up to a white house off a gravel lane a hundred yards up from Wittenberg Road. A purple rhododendron greeted us in full flower. As did the ear-splitting blast of an air horn. (A device that resembled a spray can.) "All aboard!" shouted Jim Davis, emerging from the house in a blue T-shirt that announced his loyalties: an American flag fronted by three wolves standing in prairie grass. His thick white ponytail added to his Native American appearance. He planned to drive us the rest of the way up the gravel lane in his big blue SUV. I got a kick out of his crazy energy, so I asked about the green statue of a cartoon-like cow standing beside the barn red garage.

"Does she give much milk?" I asked.

"No," he snapped. "And it tastes like Styrofoam."

But we hadn't come to trade jokes. We'd come to learn about Whispell Road. Never heard of it? Neither had I until Dave Holden told me its history. For hundreds of years, extending from Native American times through the nineteenth century, this road was one link in a Catskills crossing that's now paved over by modern roads, converted to hiking trails, or simply forgotten in the forests. A traveler from the North would have come down from Mink Hollow, crossed the eastern flank of Mount Tobias on Whispell Road, then wound south through the notch between Ticeteneyck and Tonshi out of the mountains. Today's traveler from the North would miss it all on the Thruway.

Before climbing aboard his blue Tahoe, Jim waved us into the yard, shaded by a towering white pine which drew woodpeckers to a suet feeder on its trunk, so we could peer down through a gap in the shrubs at his neighbor's garden. She'd told him that when she moved in years ago the previous owner had given her two urns filled with arrowheads dug up from the garden. "That was a flint napping spot," Jim explained. Prior to Whispell Road, this was the Blueberry Trail, a Native American route. Traveling families stopped here for a day of hunting and foraging. While the women and young men searched the mountainside for nuts and game, the older men stayed in camp to make arrowheads and stone tools.

"Slow down!" Jim shouted at a green Subaru racing up the gravel lane past his driveway. Moments later it sped back down.

"Do you get much traffic?" I asked, surprised that he got any. The lane looked like it should dead end in a few hundred yards. But it didn't.

"Frequently," Jim said. A fellow named Tepee Bob lived at the top. He had a tenant, a young woman with whom Dave had had an angry encounter last fall over the small matter of trespassing. Jim sympathized, but told us that she didn't respond well to intruders after losing her dog to a bow and arrow hunter. Besides, he advised, "She's ninety-eight pounds of fury on a Harley."

In Jim's Tahoe we headed up the lane through a shady forest of hemlocks and oaks. Normally, I'm a parker and walker on old woods roads. But I drive a Honda Insight, a low-slung hybrid that looks like it should scrape metal on speed bumps. Not Jim. If this was a road, he intended to drive it, steering sharply around pits and stones at about five miles per hour. In the back seat I bounced around as if riding an amusement park bronco. Walking would have been easier. But up front, Jim held steady to the wheel, his cigarette hand out the window. He explained that he'd first heard about Whispell Road as a boy at family gatherings.

In 1912, his great grandfather had been forced to give up a thousand-acre farm in Brown's Station, which was then flooded by the Ashokan Reservoir. For several years before 1912, though, the two youngest boys in the family had ridden a delivery wagon loaded with barrels of milk, butter, eggs, and other items on a two-day circuit linking farms in Brown's Station, Cooper Lake, and other places to the hotels in Kingston and Ellenville. On two occasions during this journey, the wagon horses had stirred up a ground hornets' nest on Whispell Road. The first time, as the horses charged down Mount Tobias to dive into Cooper Lake to salve their belly stings, the boys had jumped off the wagon for safety and instead broken bones. The second time they hung onto the wagon seat for dear life and plunged into the lake with the horses. They didn't get hurt, but they had to retrieve their barrels from the muck, an experience these men still recounted at family gatherings in their forties and fifties. Little did Jim know, back then as a boy, that he would later live at the base of Whispell Road with his partner, Betsy Stang, for what has now been twenty-two years.

Whispell Road last appeared on a map in 1898, half solid line, half dotted trail. A handful of farm houses appeared by the road. The arrival of automobiles spelled the end of Whispell Road and other rugged mountain shortcuts that could be avoided through the valleys. As far as Jim can tell from his inquiries, the town had given up its right-of-way on this route by the 1930's. In recent times, the gravel lane has been shared by a handful of property owners and, intermittently, by logging trucks. Jim, who has had a testy relationship with the loggers, blamed some of the back-seat bounciness on their heavy equipment having chewed up the road. As we ascended, we passed a few log piles left to rot. Yet the forest itself stood shady and tall. The song birds had plenty to sing about in the trees.

A century ago this mountainside had been pasture. "I've found barbed wire grown into trees that are fifty or sixty years old," Jim said. Ten minutes up the lane we reached a roadside stone wall, a remnant of the former farms. What intrigued us, though, were the cairns that stood both uphill and down, half a dozen impressive stacks up to five feet tall and five feet wide built on flat bedrock like aboveground wells. Several shorter ones had concave tops filled with fallen leaves.

What did these cairns mean? "There are a lot of theories," Jim answered. That was his polite way of saying that he and Dave disagreed. The first and least exciting explanation was that farm boys had stacked these stones while clearing fields. But the cairns looked so noble and meaningful that it seemed a shame to view them as junk piles. Jim preferred to think of those with concave tops as work tables for Native Americans, places where they'd mashed acorns and chestnuts into flour. Not Dave. He saw them as funerary objects, receptacles for bones after the deceased had been ceremoniously placed outside for vultures to pick clean.

Who was right? What I liked about the cairns was their mystery. Their meaning, once obvious to their builders, was now lost to conjecture. The woods that I saw as wild were also the ruins of earlier societies about which I knew little, be they farmers or Native Americans. In his explorations of the Woodstock Valley, Dave has found thousands of cairns left, he believes, by Native Americans, historical markers that few of us notice.

The road climbed steadily on a slope that dropped down to a creek hidden below us in the forest. We passed a solitary roadside boulder known as "Cat Rock," Jim said, after an old-time belief that bobcats or mountain lions sunned themselves on the top now growing ferns.

Farther up, he pointed to a spring box on our left, a stone-lined, trunk-sized gap in the roadside embankment. A tree root had grown across the top like a wooden handle. This spring once served a cabin to our right—Jim pointed to a stone foundation in the hemlocks.

We reached the top of the road, a small turnaround under the trees where a gated driveway curved up toward a weekend house on a spur ridge known as Roundtop. We continued straight ahead onto dirt and grass tracks that brought us into a meadow at the edge of Tepee Bob's compound. Across the field of ferns stood a small corral of metal fencing, plus a green storage-shed tent hung with a black pirate flag. A warning. But it was nice to be out in a clearing after the long drive through the woods. The ferns looked fat and feathery with summer. A *wichity-wichity-wichity* warbler sang from the edge of the field. There were a few apple trees, the descendants, Jim said, of an apple orchard planted before the American Revolution.

From here, Jim didn't know which way Whispell Road dropped down to Cooper Lake. Dave did. If I wasn't mistaken, I'd seen it on my own explorations of Mount Tobias, a deeply eroded gully that would cripple a vehicle, even Jim's SUV. If anything, given a water torrent, the gully might be a kayaker's dream. We turned around to descend. Jim drove with his head halfway out the window, his ear half-listening to our conversation. His watchfulness paid off. Near the bottom he stopped and backed up a few feet. It took me a moment to see what he'd spotted camouflaged in the brown leaves within a cluster of spindly trees on the roadside embankment, a turkey hen seated motionless on her nest. In all my walks I'd never seen such a sight. Riding high in the back seat, I'd been given a treat.

# Deep Ruts the Wagons Made

Michael Perkins

ON ONE OF THOSE golden October mornings that you wish could be bottled for sipping throughout the year, four of us set forth to explore what might have been the first road from Kingston to Woodstock, a "lost road" called Waghkonck. It starts in Stony Hollow, off Route 28 across from Hickory Barbecue.

Will Nixon and I had decided to explore old town roads. Joining us for our adventure was Will's friend Paul Levine from Connecticut, who's climbed over one hundred Catskill Peaks, and our Trailkeeper Guide, dashing Dave Holden.

We drove a quarter mile on pavement, and parked before a metal fence put up by the owners of a large gravel quarry. Dave explained that we would be passing over land owned by the Town of Kingston, a private gravel company, the Town of Woodstock, New York State, and other private owners. After crossing over a vast moonscape of a quarry, walking on the mottled bedrock of ancient sea floor, noting the striations made in it by glacial movement, we paused to admire the view before plunging into the forest and back in time to the days of bluestone quarrying. We had a panoramic view of Mount Guardian, Overlook, Ohayo Mountain, Ticeteneyck and their sisters, as well as a cell tower and a gravel grinder. Dave drew our attention to little stands of birch trees, a pioneer species that springs up in quarries. Will pointed out a healthy growth of sweet fern.

We went into the cool woods, looking for the road on which teams of horses had strained to pull wagons full of cut bluestone between the Woodstock quarries and Kingston docks. It didn't take Dave long to find it. The deep ruts made by the wagon wheels are still evident a century after the bluestone industry went bust. Four to six feet wide, it makes a pleasant path that we followed, pausing now and then to listen to our guide, as he pointed out the piles of bluestone debris beside the road, the remains of old quarries, and told us about the difficulties of cutting bluestone. Many of the quarrymen were Irish immigrants who lived with their large families in the Irish Village in Lewis Hollow. They partied hearty in their shebeens and then worked cutting and hauling the stratified Upper Devonian sandstone that would become Manhattan side-

walks. In the days before pneumatic drills, one man would hold a single edge drill while his partner would hit it with a sledge hammer. One slip, and the victim might lose his ability to support his family. For this Herculean labor, good men were paid a dollar a day in the 1880's. Woodstock was known for its flag stones for sidewalks, and for the large "platform" stones that quarry owners prized. The largest might end up in front of the Vanderbilt Mansion on Fifth Avenue.

It all ended when Portland Cement became popular. Walking along the Waghkonck Road I found myself thinking of the ghosts of the Lenni Lenape who had cut the path first. I was about to ask Dave about them when he called a stop before a cairn of stones about four feet high. Dave said it was Native American, and took out his medicine pouch to perform a tobacco ceremony—tossing pinches of Native Spirit tobacco to the Four Directions to honor the Great Spirit. Dave's Maine Indian heritage, his quirky sense of humor, and his love of and knowledge of the woods made what might have been an embarrassing New Age wannabe moment into a moving experience.

The path that had been Waghkonck road went uphill. The oaks on each side were in mast, producing masses of acorns. Dave noted this and reminded us that trees have sex. In the spring, walking through pollen in the air, we'd be walking through trees having sex. Then he added, with a mischievous smile, "How do you titillate an ocelot? You oscillate her tit a lot."

Well, you had to be there. Put experienced hikers on a new path in the woods, and they're likely to say anything. It's the camaraderie produced by mutual effort in the freedom of nature. A party of Cro-Magnon men probably shared woods tips and cracked jokes, as we were. Perhaps they even started up a marching song, as we did. I wondered if the burly, boisterous, hungover Irish drovers who urged their horses down this dry ridge road sang, when they weren't cursing? I mused, as I often do when sufficiently impressed with some evidence of what people had been capable of in the past, that these men must have been giants— almost another species—to have done what they did.

According to Alf Evers, Waghkonck or Awaghkonck, is a genuine Algonkian Indian name, meaning 'at or near a mountain.' The mountain, of course, is Overlook. When we grabbed a spot of road for a lunch break, Dave told us of his belief that Overlook was once considered a holy mountain called Manitou Mountain, and that the pre-Colonial wide Woodstock Valley had been a vast funerary site. There are thousands of cairns like the one we stopped at, and these would have been made to honor the departed—after their bodies were exposed to the elements and then their bones broken up. The Comeau Property in the center of Woodstock is at the heart of this ancient burial ground. Our town government conducts its business, Dave says, at the intersection of two ley lines: between Overlook and Mohonk, and underground streams running east to west. "I'm honored to be a member of Comeau Trailkeepers because Comeau is so special."

After a leisurely three-hour hike, the four of us emerged onto Sawkill Road and headed for Will Nixon's house opposite Kingston Reservoir Number One. Cars and trucks whizzed past us, intent on missions, missing the beauty on both sides. I wanted to turn and go back to the old lost road, where the ghosts of drovers cursing and singing behind their great horses moved through the world at a human pace. I wanted to stroll down more lost roads, looking for the past—or the eternal present?

Always the birder, Will pointed to a great blue heron lifting off. It was a good sign.

Onteora Lake, a state-owned spot popular for picnic and fishing, has a trail system that intersects in places with the Waghkonck. The entrance road is on Route 28 about five miles west of the Kingston traffic circle. —W.N.

# Camelot

Will Nixon

ON A DAMP NOVEMBER MORNING, Michael Perkins suggested a walk up Camelot Road. It seemed timely now that "Bamalot" had appeared in the headlines, updating Kennedy's "Camelot." But how did Camelot Road in the Byrdcliffe Arts Colony get its name? Michael shrugged, as we started up the lane from the Byrdcliffe Theater, a historic brown wooden building with dark windows looking closed to all but the mice for the season. "I don't know," he admitted. "Public relations, I'm sure."

From 1986 to 1994, Michael was the program director for the Woodstock Guild, which owns Byrdcliffe. On previous walks he'd shared stories that made me feel I'd missed a golden age. He'd held publishing conferences with the editor of *Publishers Weekly* (once an editor of mine), hosted a bioregional conference (once an enthusiasm of mine, though the vision of redrawing political boundaries to match watersheds seems even further from reality than it did in the early 1990's), and put on concerts, readings, and theater productions. Once, when I'd admitted that I was struggling through *The Iliad*, he'd lent me a cassette tape of a panel discussion at Byrdcliffe that included Ed Sanders reciting Homer in Greek. Where can you hear *that* anymore, I'd wondered.

But that was then. This morning the rain had ended, though a fog ceiling still hid the mountaintops. The foliage had fallen, save for rattly brown oak leaves stubbornly clinging to branches. A plastic tarp shrouded the Byrdcliffe Theater chimney for winter. The building next door, the Villetta, the original boarding house for the colony, had a sheltered front porch crowded with lawn benches and furniture. The area would be a ghost town until spring. A happy-sounding flock of chickadees had the trees to themselves.

Michael's Guild career didn't end happily. His wife, Sondra Howell, was ousted as executive director in 1994 in one of those controversies that makes Woodstock Woodstock, the little town that loves to fight. In fact, Michael hadn't walked up Camelot Road since then. I asked how it felt to be back.

"Good," he replied. "I like it." Though the loss of a beloved job must sting for years, I could tell that he'd come to savor his good memories as well as Byrdcliffe's storied past.

In 1902, Ralph Radcliffe Whitehead, a wealthy Englishman, secretly bought fifteen hundred acres of farmland on Mount Guardian's slopes to fulfill a dream shared with his wife Jane, the daughter of a Philadelphia mayor. They founded an Arts and Crafts colony, a summer community that produced fine furniture, metal work, pottery, weavings, photography, and paintings. This social experiment stood in opposition to the Industrial Revolution with its dehumanizing mass production. Within a few years the colony had constructed more than thirty buildings, most of which still remain, that resembled "low rambling Swiss chalets" with darkly stained siding, "gentle sloping roofs with wide overhangs, and ribbons of windows painted Byrdcliffe blue," as described in a walking guide flier free for the taking from a white mailbox by the theater building.

Utopian communities rarely match their ideals. The Whiteheads were aristocrats who didn't mingle with commoners in the village below. Byrdcliffe "was a happy make-believe Old England," wrote Woodstock historian Alf Evers in a preface to a brief history guide Michael authored. Ralph Whitehead "was the Lord and master, and the artists were at his beck and call." Yet several others from the colony soon came down into the valley to start the summer school of the Art Students League of New York and the Maverick Art Colony. Before 1902, Woodstock had been a farming community still lingering in its Dutch ancestry. Brydcliffe launched Woodstock as an arts colony, which remains our living tradition today. Byrdcliffe is our Mount Vernon or Monticello.

After Ralph Whitehead died in 1929, his widow Jane and their son Peter struggled for decades to pay taxes by selling off parcels of the original property. When Peter Whitehead died in 1976, he still lived in White Pines, a magnificent house that had once hosted the likes of Thomas Mann, Isadora Duncan, and many others now in the history books, but he slept under a plastic tarp that kept rainwater from dripping onto his bed. Yet he'd managed to hold onto the core of Byrdcliffe, which he bequeathed to the Woodstock Guild.

"We have a national treasure up here," Michael said. Only a few feet up Camelot Road he stopped in front of the Villetta to tell me his first story: "Wallace Stevens visited his wife here from 1915 to 1917. He wrote his long poem, 'Lettres d'un Soldat.' His wife, Elsie, was a ceramicist. She was so beautiful that she was the model for the woman on the old Mercury dime."

Now that's marrying money, I thought.

Next, we admired a darkened house down to the right, a two-story structure with attic windows peeking out from under the roof. Milton and Sally Avery had once lived here, a prominent couple in the art world from the 1920's onwards. Michael noted the second story screened-in porch. "Ralph Whitehead believed in the healthy properties of sleeping outdoors." It was one of his many ideas about what comprised the good life, which also included regular bathing, vigorous exercise, and at least two hours of manual labor each day.

Camelot Road quickly leaves the central Byrdcliffe compound. It's a private road, recently layered with fresh gravel over dirt. We passed several small cottages, then driveways leading up to houses half hidden by trees. Retaining the Byrdcliffe style, these homes looked at peace in the woods and in history. The forest trees lining the road included white pines that had dropped fresh cones gluey with sap that I kicked ahead of me like tiny footballs.

"In the Sixties thousands of hippies walked up this road to meet Bob Dylan," Michael said. "Dylan didn't like it. He moved over to Ohayo Mountain for more land and privacy." In fact, Dylan hated it. In his book *Chronicles*, he described his unwanted pilgrims as "dropouts and druggies," "moochers," and "goons" who broke into his house "at all hours of the night. At first, it was merely the nomadic homeless making illegal entry—seemed harmless enough, but then rogue radicals looking for the Prince of Protest began to arrive—unaccountable-looking characters, gargoyle-looking gals, scarecrows, stragglers looking to party, raid the pantry."

This morning, the former Dylan house has been overtaken by a different crew, workmen who've filled the well-groomed gravel driveway with shiny pickup trucks and vans, an orange port-a-san, a blue-tarp storage tent, and, back behind a garage, stacks of sky-blue foam boards that I guessed might be insulation. A table saw whined, a radio thumped classic rock. The long low-roofed building on the far side was a country estate undergoing renovations. "I don't even recognize the place," Michael said. In the 1970's he could have bought it himself for $80,000, a dilapidated piece of history that Joan Baez had once described as haunted. He declined. "The heating costs alone would have broken me." Instead, Wall Streeters bought the house and invested heavily in renovations. Now a different rock star lives there, one who doesn't draw idolatrous fans.

Yet not everything changes. Before the driveway, a small brook slips under the road and sluices down the hillside into a half-circle pool held back by a cement dam. This morning it looked metallic with its shimmering black and white reflections of cloud light and tree shadows. "That's the Bob Dylan swimming pool," Michael said. Once, after camping out for two nights with his nephew, they'd finished their journey by jumping in. "It was very refreshing. Warm, too."

A bit farther to the left, we passed the turnoff to the Mount Guardian trail, a path not found on hiking maps but well trod by locals. I'd climbed it many times myself. The route wends its way up through the forest of chestnut oaks and mountain laurels, then zig-zags several times and comes out of the shrubs to a rock outcropping with a secluded but marvelous view of the Woodstock Valley below. Years ago, Michael had led his wife, Sondra, up to this lookout. He'd told her, "Someday all this will be yours." A year later, by fate or by chance, it was, when she became the Guild's executive director in 1984.

Several times, I've continued up from this outcropping to find the summit of Mount Guardian, which does, in fact, exist, though I've never reached it without thrashing around for an inordinate length of time in mountain laurels, a woody bush that is a master at tripping, entangling, and thwapping you in the face. Trust me, the summit isn't worth it. Yet in June nothing can be prettier in Woodstock than walking the Mount Guardian path when these demonic bushes have transformed themselves into angels laden with pink and white bunches of flowers. It's as if the forest has staged a wedding for itself.

This morning, though, we stuck to Camelot Road. The gravel continued over the gently rolling terrain to reach two final houses down to the right, both newer than Byrdcliffe but blended into the forest with rustic shingle siding. The gravel road curved down into the last driveway, while the original Camelot Road continued straight onto hard ground with a moss carpet and parallel ruts lined with fallen leaves. Yet this simple fork in the road was more significant than it looked.

Michael and I had given ourselves the assignment of exploring Woodstock's "lost roads." We'd started on the Waghkonck Road, perhaps the first route from Kingston to Woodstock, which had appeared on nineteenth century maps, but vanished by the age of the automobile. Not so for Camelot Road. At this junction, our society had decided long after the arrival of cars to let a road revert back to the wild. Though I may be an eco-pessimist, places like this give me hope. The first tree trunk fallen across the route served as our gateway to a lost road, or, at least a lost road in the making.

We entered the hemlocks to dip down across a stream, then continued the gentle ascent. By now Michael was musing aloud about Jane Whitehead who'd lived long past her husband until she died at ninety in 1955. In the 1930's as a widow, she'd brought young Father Francis to preside over the small wooden chapel near the top of Meads Mountain Road. On Sundays she'd traveled Camelot Road to attend to her spiritual needs. If I was going to church, I decided, I'd want to pass through hemlocks, too. They have a dimly lit, mysterious atmosphere that reminds me of Gothic cathedrals. Sometimes I fancy gnomes hidden among hemlocks spying on me with impish amusement. Surely, Jane Whitehead sensed spirits in these woods of her own choosing.

After hopping across a second stream, we climbed out into open woodlands filled with gray sky. Meads Mountain Road was in the near distance. For years, driving down Overlook Mountain, I'd noticed an old woods road that comes up alongside a small field to intersect with the pavement. I'd always wondered where it led, but never enough to pull over and explore. Why not? The rush of the automobile, I suppose. The time pressures of life. The vanity of having hiked Overlook Mountain, which seemed more impressive than these abandoned wheel ruts down into the woods. But now I'd walked Camelot Road, as inconspicuous as it might be at this end. Michael and I reached the pavement. We turned around and walked right back into the forest.

A friend showed me the Mount Guardian Trail. Since then, I've introduced it to others. For better or worse, having a guide may still be the best way to learn this path. Lower down, it has blazes. Higher up in the mountain laurel, the path is tramped. But it has turnoffs to nowhere. The top, at least what I consider the top, is a rock outcropping well below the summit. But it has a great view of the valley.

This trail doesn't appear on maps. Nor do I know of a good description that gives distances. If you're feeling adventurous, try it. I park at the Brydcliffe

Theater on Upper Brydcliffe Road and walk up Camelot Road for about a quarter mile. A small sign on the left announces the Mount Guardian Trail. Cross the clearing to the woods road on the far side. It curves through the woods, crosses a wooden bridge, then ramps up a steep pitch. Keep your eyes open. The blazed trail branches off to the right. The path should be clear, though it does have confusing turnoffs. –W.N.

||||||||||||||||||||||||||||||||||||||||||||||||||||||||||||||||||||||||||||||||||||||||||||||||||||||||||||||||||||||||||||||||||||||||||||||||||||||||||||||

# Climbing Mount Guardian

Michael Perkins

In late June I climbed
               Mount Guardian,
Hoping when I reached the summit
I might somehow keep on climbing.
On my way up a snake slid
Across my path and stopped,
Curved like a hook, to watch me pass:
A sign, I hoped, that I was
Still welcome in those green woods.
Higher up, the mountain laurel
Spread in pink bloom everywhere.
Below me the wide Woodstock Valley
Lay half in shadow, half in light.
A fly my sole companion,
I stood on a boulder near the top
Stretching up to the noon sun,
Shrinking in mountain perspective
All the little lives I led below.
Hawks swooped, an eagle passed,
And I felt stab the glad ache
In my shoulder blades where
                  wings would start.

# Danger on the Trail

Michael Perkins

FEBRUARY, THE DEAD OF WINTER. To the Romans, who named it, the month of purification. To the Anglo-Saxons, it was "mud month." Waist-high snowbanks, below-zero temperatures. Groundhogs who want to stay snug irritably bite mayors, and mice come in the house to get warm. Cabin fever brings on the megrims.

It was time for a hike. Time for those intrepid perambulators Nixon and Perkins to continue their exploration of the "lost roads" around Woodstock. Will Nixon suggested trekking Silver Hollow, so one morning the two of us set forth in Will's Honda Insight out Route 212 to Silver Hollow Road, where we drove down a dirt road packed with snow to a dead end at a Rod and Gun club. We would hike the road in the notch and emerge on Route 214, then hike back. It was familiar territory to me because it was near the Devil's Path and the Devil's Tombstone, where I'd done an epic marathon hike years before.

We stepped out of the car and pulled on cleats over our boots, sipping the cold, crisp air. We headed expectantly to the trail head, gazes fixed on the white capped mountains ahead. Oops! Snow so deep it was up to our knees. What kind of winter hikers were we to assume that a lost road would be plowed? Sheepishly, we returned to the car to consider Plan B. I suggested the rail trail that runs from Hurley to High Falls along Route 209. It was sure to be passable without snowshoes, and I argued that it counted as a lost road because of its history. Known officially as the D&H Canal Heritage Corridor, it began as a link in the Delaware & Hudson Canal system that brought anthracite coal from Pennsylvania to Eddyville on the Hudson from 1828 to 1898. When the D&H became a railroad, mules pulling canal boats were replaced by steam locomotives. Eventually the railroad stopped, weeds took over the tracks, and a vital "road" became lost—until it was converted to a walking and biking trail courtesy of a 1986 New York State Grant.

On our way out Route 28 to Hurley a car pulled out in front of us, forcing Will to jam on the brakes. I cursed, but he remained calm. I reflected on how much safer walking is than driving, and the psychological benefits that accrue—among them, an equable temperament.

Then, as we were approaching our destination, Will told me a story about an incident on the Heritage Corridor Trail some time ago.

Will is a staunch environmentalist. He's worked as a journalist in the field, and has served on the boards of environmental organizations. He told me he was taking a walk on the trail one evening when he heard the sound hikers dread: all-terrain vehicles growling loudly, coming at him. (Motorized vehicles are banned on the Heritage Corridor.)

"I decided to stand my ground. They had to stop, and they were angry. One of them attacked me, hitting me with his fists on the back of my head. I was pushed to the ground as he cursed at me."

One would not suspect looking at gentle, affable Will that he could be so temerarious. My admiration for him, already high, shot up. This was a battle-scarred tree hugger I was hanging with.

He went to the nearby State Police Barracks, and the police went off in pursuit of the ruffians, but to no avail. They made him go to the hospital, but he was okay.

We parked in a lot just south of Hurley, where the trail sign said "No Motorized Vehicles," and started off on a 3.1 mile walk on a well maintained straight trail through the woods. I found myself listening for the sound of ATVs, but all I heard was highway noise coming from Route 209. If one roared up to us, I wouldn't block its way, although I might cock a disapproving eyebrow—a tactic which, while devastating in bar fights, might be lost on the kind of insensitive hoople who thinks of forest paths as racetracks.

We encountered no one. We strode down an utterly straight snowy path, low ridges on our left, on our right highway, then a house, then declivities. The world was white, the sky was overcast, the path was...boring. It presented no challenges. Come spring, it would be lovely to walk at a brisk pace to High Falls, checking out the budding leaves and wild flowers and birds; but now my mind wandered. (This is a bad sign. A good hike presents enough difficulties that your mind has no time for its usual tricks—miss an exposed root in your path, risk a sprained ankle.)

As happens so often, a book came to mind, and to our rescue. (At least to mine. Will was striding ahead, looking this time like he might lie down in front of an ATV if one should come along.)

The book was the *The Compleat Angler* by Izaak Walton and Charles Cotton. It is a discourse on fishing, published in 1653. But it is also one of the great books about walking, for in it friends cruise the English countryside looking for places to fish, enjoying being outdoors, and looking for an inn where they might grab some victuals and a beer.

When I suggested to Will that we should turn around, heed our stomachs, and head for lunch, he was immediately amenable. With no ATVs to confront, I guess he too considered it a lost day.

And that, dear reader, is how we ended up having lunch at the nearby Hurley Mountain Inn, which began its existence as a hostelry in the early nineteenth century. As Izaak Walton recommends, we enjoyed "good discourse" and planned our next venture up a "lost road."

|||||||||||||||||||||||||||||||||||||||||||||||||||||||||||||||||||||||||||||||||||||||||||
Michael grew bored. I was assaulted. That doesn't mean that others don't enjoy the rail trail. In fact, I've taken many pleasant walks on this path that passes through surprisingly wild areas. We parked at the trailhead lot on Route 209 several miles south of the Kingston traffic circle and just before reaching Gill's Farm. -W.N.
|||||||||||||||||||||||||||||||||||||||||||||||||||||||||||||||||||||||||||||||||||||||||||

# Following the Black Line

Will Nixon

CALL ME A CYNIC. The very word "mall" conjures up *Dawn of the Dead*, George Romero's zombie classic about blue-skinned dullards lumbering around a mall that continues to function with bright lights, water fountains, and overhead Muzak and shopping announcements despite the fact that nobody is alive to run the place. (I'll confess to a fondness for zombies. I've written a poetry chapbook inspired by *Night of the Living Dead*.) Now and again I sneak down to the Hudson Valley Mall for a rocking Hollywood movie with guns, babes, and explosions, but I tend not to talk about it publicly.

When Michael Perkins suggested we join the mall walkers for a morning, I knew he was right. Sometimes nothing is better than putting aside your cherished prejudices to experience life afresh. Besides, our previous walk in search of a "lost road" had ended after twenty feet as we trudged up to our shins in snow and realized that lost roads weren't plowed. Maybe the mall made sense in winter.

I picked up Michael who'd dressed dapperly for the occasion, not in his usual wools and walking stick, but in a brown bomber jacket and brown leather hat. His red scarf looked like an ascot. I'd pulled on my boots and blue fleece jacket, same as always. Hiking let me indulge my dull style.

The mall opens its food court doors at 6 a.m. We arrived at the more civilized hour of 8:30. (The stores don't open until 10.) A dozen cars had already parked in that corner of the lot, plus a food delivery truck unloading boxes outside a restaurant with dark windows. At least it had windows. Most of the mall we'd circled had blank bunker-like walls as if the sprawling building had no front, only a rear on all sides. It looked well defended against everything but the recession.

Michael paused to read the "Behavior Code" sign on the outdoor pillar by the food court doors. The sign failed to warn us that writers were considered a security threat. On a subsequent visit I was confronted by two mall security men within minutes of taking out my notepad and pen, and led up to the management office in the cinder block bowels of the building, far from the shiny hallways. JoAnn Hickman, the mall's gracious marketing director, later apologized for the confusion.

Inside the food court Michael and I saw a handful of older people scattered about the white grid of tables. They'd found takeout coffees to nurse even though the metal grates for Vitamin World and the other shops remained closed. As always, the mall seemed alien to me, a consumerist space station. The air smelled sugary, the intercom played an Eddie Vedder rock song too loudly, the skylights cast a glow that seemed fluorescent even if natural, the plants by the pillars looked rubbery and indestructible. I'd rather sit in the Bread Alone bakery for my morning coffee. But Michael and I had come on assignment. Across the food court we reached a wide hallway. A sales kiosk for eyeglasses was closed for the night with a gray tarp pulled tight around it like an industrial-strength shower curtain.

How would we recognize a mall walker? Several people passed by, but I suspected that they worked here, especially the woman pushing a gray garbage bin on clackity wheels. Certainly, she wasn't doing that for the exercise. I began to fear that we were chasing an urban legend. Sure, mall walkers were a funny idea, at least to a pair of self-proclaimed rustic ramblers like us, but did people really come here just to walk? We headed down the hallway, passing glass storefronts for DVDs or jeans. The mannequins, I noticed, were dressed for spring.

"There's one," Michael said. "I saw the white tennis shoes." We'd reached an intersection with another hallway catty-corner to ours. I'd glimpsed her myself, a woman in jeans with short gray hair who'd darted around a corner at the end of her hallway, which ended at J.C. Penny's glass doors. But how did we know she wasn't simply window shopping?

Michael and I chose a different hallway, one straight to our left. Now I saw this woman walking back in our direction, acting like she was on a mission. She strode down the single row of black tiles that decorate the perimeter of the white hallway as if following a path. After she rounded the corner and caught up with us, I popped the question: "Are you a mall walker?"

She gave me a puzzled look. Maybe "mall walker" wasn't the right term. Or I'd sounded dubious. Yet she turned out to be friendly, as walkers invariably are, so she explained that she walked the mall three mornings a week, following the black line through all the halls, a track eight-tenths of a mile long. She does two laps for a workout that takes half an hour. "My doctor is after me to exercise," she said.

Now that we'd met one, we soon saw a dozen: older men and women, mostly walking alone at their various speeds, yet nodding back and forth in camaraderie. Some were on the younger side of old age, thin and light-footed in jeans, sweatshirts, and sneakers that squeaked on the tiles. Others were elderly. "I can't stop," said one burly fellow in a blue shirt and jeans whose red suspenders caught my eye. I walked alongside, as he pushed ahead with arms swinging wide. "I've got a bad back, bad legs, and bad feet," he said. Yet he walked every morning. "It makes me feel better." In contrast, a white haired woman in headphones almost seemed to be skipping. She swung her arms together so that her hands touched, karaoke clapping to music only she heard. She'd tied her winter jacket around her waist like a girl.

Michael and I sat on a bench to interview the passers-by. Larry Dachenhausen of Ruby told us that he had a breathing disorder, which I heard in the shallow gasps in his voice. In the past he walked along roads or at Dietz Stadium, but he'd grown too sensitive to carbon monoxide and road salt. "In this area the mall is probably the best environment," he said. "It's cool in the summer, warm in the winter."

"Do you miss the birds and the flowers?" Michael asked.

"No," he said. "I've got them in my yard."

A gregarious older guy in a red and black checked wool jacket and Red Sox cap plopped down on the bench beside Michael. "I've got two new knees," he said, patting his blue trousers. "Two new shoulders. A pacemaker. And I've had a bypass."

"My God," Michael said. "You're the bionic man."

"That's right," he said. He was Lenny Robinson from Hurley, retired after driving a tractor-trailer for forty years. Now he walked in the mornings, worked at Friendly's for a few hours, and went home.

Not everyone was elderly. Mary Metty of Ulster Park still had shortish cinnamon blonde hair. A few years ago she'd begun walking here to lose weight after dropping her kids off at high school at 8 a.m. "It worked," she said, now looking fit and content in her white sweater. She admired the older people. "There was one lady who was half walking, half limping. Yet when I started, she outwalked me, three laps to my two."

By now I'd decided that mall walkers were the anti-zombies. They were people who refused to succumb to old age, bad knees, winter weather, or the other obstacles that stand in the way of our bipedal nature. Rather than scorning the mall, they humanized it, adopting it to their needs. As I learned from JoAnn Hickman, the marketing director, there are several dozen regulars, including a ninety-three year old, a few grandmothers who push baby carriages, and one die-hard who does laps both in mornings and evenings. "We get to know them," she said. She'd just called one who'd been in the hospital. She's done promotions with free T-shirts and free pedometers. At the customer service counter, I took a flier for "WalkHVM," a program sponsored by the mall, WellCare, and Benedictine Hospital that hosts monthly gatherings in the food court with free bagels and speakers on health issues. From her and several other mall employees, I sensed great affection for the mall walkers, an elderly but determined pedestrian tribe.

Michael and my favorites turned out to be a pair of love birds from Lake Katrine, Betty and Joe Eliching, who at eighty-one and eighty-four have been walking the mall since it opened in 1981. Bashful to be interviewed, they charmed me with both their long marriage and their dedication. To them, the heyday of mall walking had passed years ago. "We've seen many people drop out," Joe said. "Now we're the veterans." In the past, they walked two or three laps, but now they settled for one at their own sweet pace. The only problem was the hard floor tiles. They recommended Rockport or New Balance as the best shoes. After wishing us a good morning, they continued along the black line.

"Strangely enough, that gave me a lift," Michael said at the end of our visit. Formerly a skeptic, he now praised the mall for helping to keep people alive. "That poor guy with two knee replacements, two shoulder replacements, a pacemaker—he needs this place," he said. Nor did Michael leave with me. His wife Sondra would come down in a few hours to join him for a movie. For now he headed to the food court. He'd brought a good book to read.

# Walking Ashokan Shores

Michael Perkins

EVERY YEAR through the 1990's I celebrated the arrival of spring by walking from my house in Glenford to Kingston along Route 28. I wanted to stretch my legs and prove a point: that you could move between towns without a car.

I like road walking. I confess to a feeling of superiority to people stuck in the cars that sped past. As I walked, I imagined a slower time, when curvy Old Route 28 was the road between Kingston and the West. Stretches of this "lost road" loop away from Route 28, built in the 1950's, and offer glimpses of a quieter time.

Route 28 rolls past New York City land, a buffer between 28 and the Ashokan Reservoir. One early May morning I decided to make my journey to Kingston not on the noisy highway, but on the abandoned railroad tracks that run parallel to the road on DEP land.

It was magical, stepping high over the rotting railroad ties and the weeds that stretched for miles through the woods.

The twelve-square miles of the Ashokan Reservoir are bounded by a rocky shoreline that is forty miles long; it curves like a bent fishhook through our landscape. At its full capacity of one hundred and twenty-seven billion gallons, Ashokan is up to two-hundred-feet deep in the center. It is three miles across, but if you are out in a boat in the middle of a summer day it seems wider. Ashokan is fed by the Esopus and Schoharie Creeks, as well as by the thousands of trickles, rivulets, brooks, and streams in its nine-hundred-square mile watershed. It is home to brown and rainbow trout, as well as smallmouth bass and walleye. In times of drought, when the Catskills don't receive their usual forty-four inches of rain and snow, reservoir levels may sink to twenty-five percent of capacity, which happened in the 1960's. At such times the stone foundations of the farmhouses and villages that were razed to make way for the reservoir become visible, tombstones at the bottom of a drinkable sea.

This is Ashokan, or "place of many fishes."

Eight centuries before the Christian Era the short, slender, olive skinned people who called themselves Lenni Lenape hunted and fished and took shelter from storms in rock caves on slopes above the waters of the sparkling Esopus, which ran where Ashokan is now. When the Dutch, and then English settlers arrived, eight thousand Lenni Lenape lived here. None remain.

The Ashokan Reservoir was built between 1903 and 1917 by an M.I.T. trained engineer named J. Waldo Smith. It took over two thousand workmen, mostly Italian and Irish immigrants, to accomplish this wonder, at a cost of $30 million and many lives lost. Two thousand people were displaced after living here for two centuries.

Because New York City owns Ashokan, whenever I walk its shoreline I think of people in Manhattan, where I spent my young manhood, blithely drinking and bathing in the waters of this inexhaustible fountain.

Those who drive around the reservoir on Route 28A or cross it on Reservoir Road south of Route 28 in Shokan know of the grand views. You can park the car and walk paved routes closed to traffic. If you're crossing on Reservoir Road, take a left onto 28A at the end. Continue east on 28A for two miles to a sign for public parking on the left. This half-mile road leads to a round parking circle. From here you may walk for a mile and a quarter on the embankment. At the end, you'll reach the Reservoir Road intersection. If you want to walk further, continue across to the road closed by barriers. This stretch on the Olive Bridge Dam is two miles long. Keep your eyes open for bald eagles, which nest in the area.
−W.N.

# The Knight Tower

Will Nixon

FOR A FINE VIEW of the Ashokan Reservoir, you can't beat Barry Knight's fire tower amid the pine trees and oaks on a bluestone ledge behind his house on Route 28A in Hurley. Rather than an enclosed cab, the top is a cedar deck with railings and a three-hundred-and-sixty-degree view of the Shawangunks, Catskills, and nine miles of the reservoir that's nearly thirteen miles long. He can count twenty-two other towers from his perch, including cell towers, transmission towers, a water tower, and the sentinel-like stone tower on the Shawangunk Ridge. With powerful 10x30 binoculars he can see people climbing the Overlook Mountain fire tower. East of Overlook, beyond small slumped hills, he points to a pinkish dot in the valley haze that's Olana, Frederic Church's mansion across the Hudson. He can identify twenty-four prominent Catskill peaks, including the great wall of summits at the western end of the reservoir. At night he sees countless stars, though when he holds his *Peterson* guide overhead, they all match up with the star charts. As the seasons pass from spring to fall he observes the pine cones bunched in nearby tree tops maturing from green to brown. When he first saw the brilliant colors of the scarlet tanagers and cedar waxwings that perch high in trees he couldn't believe that he hadn't noticed them before. Several times a wildlife rehabilitator has released hawks and owls from his tower after they've recovered from injuries. Once an ornithologist called in a barred owl with her owl vocalizations, a dry-throated rasping that also sounds like zombies. Another time Barry was left speechless with awe for ten minutes after hearing a local fiddler play "Ashokan Farewell" in view of the reservoir at sunset. He has has invited hundreds of visitors to share the Knight Tower experience, and welcomes more. "When people look out, their faces open up," he says. "Their eyes open, their mouths open. It's hard for them to leave." Even the man so afraid of heights that he sat on the top step hugging the railing enjoyed what he saw.

We all have our fantasies. I'll confess that Barry Knight has fulfilled one of mine: to have a fire tower as your elevated back deck. What impresses me further is that he's not by nature a builder or an engineer. Before erecting this forty-three-foot-tall steel structure largely by himself, his only previous project was constructing the green shed that stands in the trees below the tower. Yet he loved becoming a middle-aged builder. "I couldn't wait to get up here in the morning," he says. He sat at his picnic table by the shed and puzzled through the next step in the process, which often entailed rigging up ropes and pulleys from the trees to hoist the metal beams into place in the air. Rather than feeling intimidated or incompetent, he felt challenged, even euphoric when his mind had "Eureka!" moments with the answers. "I wish everyone could have a challenge like this," he says. "It teaches you what you can do."

In 2002 he retired from his career in color printing. Already a volunteer fire tower steward on Overlook Mountain, he overheard a conversation one day about abandoned fire towers and decided to get one for himself. Through contacts he reached Martin Podskoch, author of *Fire Towers of the Catskills: Their History and Lore*, who put him in touch with Al Moulin, an older gentleman in Esperance, who'd taken possession of a tower that had come down from Petersburg Mountain in Schoharie County in 1999. Al Moulin, too, dreamed of raising a fire tower in his field, but age had gotten the better of him. The metal structure lay in pieces in mud and grass. Barry recalls their conversation: "I said, 'How much do you want for it?' He said, 'My wife wants me to get it out of here.'" Barry visited Esperance eight times to meet Al Moulin and figure out how to reassemble the metal bars and bolts scattered in grass. Finally, he trucked the pieces home to Hurley. He also had Benson Steel in Saugerties make thirteen replacement parts.

Because the metal had oxidized over the years, he had to clean, prime, and coat each piece with aluminum paint. (Today the tower, standing on four round cement supports, looks new.) During football season, he cleaned hundreds of bolts recovered from the mud with a wire brush while watching TV. In 2004 he began erecting the tower bar by bar, then level by level. Each step posed new questions, forcing him to devise ways to hoist and secure each beam by himself. For one corner, the tree for the rope and pulley system stood down in the field below the bluestone ledge. In July 2006 he finished. Yet before he did, he had a remarkable moment. Now fifty-eight he's lived in the same spot for most of his life. (In 1973 he moved from the front to the back house on adjacent land parcels.) Yet the day he reached the top level of the tower and sat on a board before beginning to install the deck, he looked out over the tree canopy for the first time. "I slowly stood up," he recalls, ignoring the forty-foot drop beneath his feet. "I couldn't believe what I saw. My eyes were so open. I never knew what the view would be like. When I got up for the first time, what a moment that was." Now he enjoys sharing the experience with others. The other day a Japanese couple climbed the tower. In their excitement they spoke Japanese. Barry couldn't understand a word they were saying. Yet he didn't need to. He knew what they felt standing on his sky deck for the heaven-on-earth views.

# THE GREATER CATSKILLS:

## Lost and Found in
## the Blue Mountains

# Walking in Ashokan

Michael Perkins

BEFORE I CAME TO ASHOKAN, I had no place in the world. Even after I bought a house on its northern shore, I expected that life would someday take me elsewhere. But I have lived here for nearly three decades, and it is a new century. I have traveled far enough walking in Ashokan.

How I came to the Hudson River Valley happened this way: I followed a faithless woman to the blue mountains, and could not leave them even after she left me.

How I came to feel that Ashokan was home happened this way: one night, after sitting with strangers in a crowded, brightly lighted room, I walked three and a half miles up our steep mountain road, absorbed in solitary reverie. It was past midnight in late September. My way was lighted by a nearly full moon and a profligate scattering of stars. When I began to descend the south slope of Ohayo Mountain, I was astonished by the immense lake that shimmered on the valley floor below. The Ashokan Reservoir was a magnificent eye reflecting everything, large enough to mirror the universe. It would suffice for a world.

# Sold

Will Nixon

FIVE YEARS EARLIER, the brick apartment building on East 47th Street had been a great find, offering us a cozy fifth-floor perch in a block otherwise dominated by steel and glass high-rises. But now I'd burned out on life. So much had gone wrong. My father-in-law had died of cancer, a man dear to me who belonged in a Saul Bellow novel for his feisty mix of intellectual chops and earthy humor. He was a bank economist who read *Rolling Stone* for its politics. Then I'd been fired from a magazine job I should have quit a year earlier. Among the warning signs I'd ignored was a fight with the managing editor after I caught her rewriting quotations to sound better. Yet she'd been smart enough to leave for a summer lighthouse job. I hung around and got canned. Now I was freelancing, earning a pittance of what was needed to survive in midtown. My wife was carrying the burden. Sometimes I woke up too early, just after dawn, and heard a melodious song outside our window. A house finch? Or a fancy car horn? What I longed for? Or what I loathed? After failing to fall back asleep, I shuffled out to our kitchen alcove to sip my coffee while staring at the YMCA window across the street. Opened several inches it revealed a young man in the shower soaping his groin. There had to be a better life.

Then came my break: a magazine assignment from *Mother Jones* to investigate shrimp farms destroying the coastal mangroves in Ecuador. The shrimp ponds, which resembled wastewater lagoons, earned fantastic profits but eliminated mangroves, the crucial fish nurseries that supported local villages. Though it received little coverage, this story paralleled the clear-cutting of rain forests. (In the dozen years since writing the article, I haven't regained my appetite for shrimp.) On an all-night bus ride up to Quito in the Andes, a trip around hairpin turns that offered window views down the plunging mountainside, I distracted myself by reading a book by Rick Bass, an enchanting writer from the Yaak Valley of Montana, a wilderness on the back side of nowhere. (To stay awake as he swung his school bus-like bus around the curves, the driver played jackhammer salsa and rap. Surely, I was the only passenger who understood English, for the rap lyrics were Triple-X. I couldn't imagine the grandmotherly woman seated ahead of me with a live chicken in her purse enjoying "pussy" rhymes.) In his short stories Rick Bass created characters as mythic as Paul Bunyan frontiersmen yet as tenderhearted as punch-drunk lovers. This wasn't the work of an alienated urban sophisticate. This book captured the wonders of the wilds. Somewhere in the middle of it, perhaps while glancing down from a hairpin turn into the black void, I decided that upon returning to Manhattan I'd rent a cabin in the Catskills. To hell with being a freelance environmental journalist stuck on East 47th Street. I wanted to step out my front door into the wilderness.

Easier said than done, of course. For one, I had a marriage. For another, I'd never done anything so bold, impetuous, or crazy, at least not since college when I'd been a philosophy major, a ski bum, etc. (What was college for, if not to change your life every six months?) Though the fall and into the winter, I dithered and dutifully attended couple's counseling. My wife, who viewed East 47th Street as our first comfortable apartment together, believed that I wanted out of our marriage. I persisted in claiming that I didn't want to leave her, but did want a getaway cabin. In February I finally called a real estate agent in Phoenicia, a number given me by a friend who had a weekend house in the Catskills.

"I have the perfect place for you," said Rick Ricciardella, an affable man on the phone, after I'd told him my dream of renting a writer's cabin in the woods. "The only problem is, you can't get to it."

Of course, I shouldn't admit to choosing my future home at that moment, not sight unseen, not on my first call to a real estate agent. So I took another step. After clearing my desk in Manhattan, I unfolded my Catskills hiking map to confirm my hunch that I knew the cabin's location. Rick had mentioned Panther Kill Road. If that lay below Panther Mountain, I had a story to tell.

Back in January, Rick explained, a torrential rainstorm had dumped four inches of warm rain on a snowpack up to six feet deep in the mountains, causing massive flooding. Both bridges into Phoenicia had been under water. Stream banks had ripped loose, a major road had washed out, several tractor-trailers had bounced down the roaring rapids like boxcar canoes. Amid the damage, the small footbridge to the rental cabin had washed away. Otherwise, it sounded like my dream: a log cabin with a wood stove nestled in a hemlock grove. "The last renter wrote a children's book," Rick added, "but you can't get there now."

I knew that snowpack. After Christmas, I'd taken the bus from Manhattan with a friend to go camping. Over two nights we intended to hike a twenty-mile loop over four mountains, starting with Panther. In summer this trip would be an overnighter, but with the snow to slow us down, we gave ourselves an extra day. From the bus window, though, the roadside snow looked so patchy that we wondered if the snowshoes strapped to our packs would be dead weight.

We needn't have worried. At the trail start, we met a young family tobogganing down the path. We didn't climb much higher than their toboggan chute before stopping, already winded and sweaty in the knee-deep snow, to strap on our snowshoes for what turned out to be one of the hardest backpacks of my life.

That afternoon we only covered a mile before the hour grew late enough for us to choose a spot that we stomped level with our snowshoes for a tent site. We changed into puffy parkas, booties, and other warm clothes that made us into walking sleeping bags. Fortunately, my finicky stove worked in the cold. We had an endless supply of feathery snow to melt into water for hot drinks and dehydrated dinners. My spaghetti and meatballs actually tasted like spaghetti and meatballs.

Then the trees started cracking. After each loud snap, we looked around to see which one had fallen, but we couldn't spot any newly split trunks.

"Do you think one could fall on our tent?" my friend asked.

Yes, I thought, half a dozen could fall on our tent. But we were stuck in the middle of the woods. Where else could we camp?

After a while we decided that the forest was fooling us. Despite the sharp noises, no trees had broken. The forest was merely cracking its knuckles. By the time we crawled into our sleeping bags, we felt reassured that we wouldn't wake up under a log. It was well after dark, almost six o'clock. Now the challenge was lying for twelve hours in our bags without getting so restless we had trouble sleeping. My friend rolled around for much of the night, but I felt well rested by dawn. At one point, though, I'd peeked through my nose hole to find my frozen breath hanging like a dewy pull chain from the tent seam inches above my head. Winter camping had its mysteries.

The next day was tough. We had to break trail in deep powder, which, even on snowshoes, felt like trudging with ankle weights through loose sand. Twice we reached the summit of Panther Mountain, only to learn that we'd reached the false summit of Panther Mountain. The next frosted hump waited far up the ridge. Not until mid-afternoon did we reach the true summit, hungry and tired. Our canteens had iced up, so we had to bang the lids against trees to unscrew them. In my lunch bag I discovered that even Triskets could freeze. My friend had been sweating so heavily under his backpack that his nylon shell wore a sheen of black ice.

For our labors, however, we were rewarded with a winter wonderland. The snow-caked balsam trees resembled Snow Queens in flared ballroom dresses. They pointed long fingers in every direction. Many raised small white crosses as crowns. In the gaps between trees a snowshoe hare had hopped around, leaving V-shaped footprints, nature's elegant version of our plodding snowshoes. I hadn't felt so immersed in snow in almost twenty

years, not since college ski bumming in the High Sierras. I was in the wild. I loved it. The only disappointment was being stuck in a cloud that teased us with fleeting glimpses of the valley below.

That night we camped in a col half a mile down from the top. This time, the trees were quiet, but a constant wind funneled across this low spot in the ridge. The tree trunks had snow stripes like stocking seams blown on their windy side. In the moonlight they were an exotic sight. I know, because this time my bladder didn't hold until morning. When I later crawled out to start breakfast, I saw that I'd been shivering so hard under the moon and stars that my pee hole had carved a Chinese hieroglyphic in the snow.

Our final day was our reward. A gorgeous blue sky. The sun warm enough to make icicles drip. Our gloves dried out. Our canteens unscrewed. Best of all, we enjoyed this thaw by lounging on Giant Ledge, which had sweeping views of the Catskills from nearby Slide Mountain, tallest in the Catskills, to Overlook Mountain above Woodstock. Even though hundreds of people lived in this viewshed we could see nothing but winter forest from the wooded valleys to the frosted summits. The Catskills performed the rare feat of incorporating people and wilderness into the same landscape.

By now we'd abandoned as totally crazy our original plan of hiking three more mountains, so we took the shortcut down to Woodland Valley. Only in the final mile did we meet another pair of backpackers, who were hiking our route in the opposite direction. They'd camped the previous night on a hillside above houses in the valley.

"It was terrible," one said. "The coyotes kept the dogs barking half the night."

Did I feel jealous! I was nearly forty years old, yet I'd heard coyotes only once in my life. I'd lived too long with the garbage truck compacters, pneumatic drills, and the other wailings and groanings of Manhattan. Even in winter I ran the apartment window fan at night for its white noise.

For a moment, I considered suggesting that we camp an extra night in the woods. In this snowy stillness we'd hear the coyotes howling from anywhere in this valley. But my friend had cut his hand slicing cold hard cheese. And we were less than an hour from the road, then the bus ride home to hot showers and warm apartments. Shouldering our packs, we continued down.

On the hiking map now spread on my desk two months later I saw that the Panther Kill was, indeed, a stream that flowed from a steep bowl on the flank of Panther Mountain. We'd glimpsed that valley through the mist. What more did I need to know?

One thing.

Yes," said Rick when I called back. "There are plenty of bears."

||||||||||||||||||||||||||||||||||||||||||||||||||||||||||||||||||||||||||||||

There's no reason to undertake a winter expedition to visit Giant Ledge. In fact, it may be my favorite short hike in the Catskills, a mile and a half by trail from the trailhead parking area at the hairpin turn on Route 47 about seven and a half miles south of Route 28 in Big Indian. –W.N.

||||||||||||||||||||||||||||||||||||||||||||||||||||||||||||||||||||||||||||||

# Lost

Will Nixon

MY GIRLFRIEND DIDN'T UNDERSTAND why I was cutting our weekend short to snowshoe alone up Southwest Hunter Mountain, which had no trail, no views, nothing to recommend it. The top was notoriously difficult to find: an orange canister nailed to a tree somewhere in the middle of acres of spruce and fir trees on the long ridge that was, in fact, a spur of Hunter Mountain, rather than a peak in its own right. If not for the Catskill 3500 Club, which included Southwest Hunter on its list of thirty-five peaks that aspirants needed to climb, who'd bother? Yet I had to do it. I'd chosen the mountain over her. I didn't care.

On Sunday morning, I woke early and kissed my girlfriend good-bye in bed. Drowsy from migraine medicine, she hugged me weakly and wished me luck. Neither of us wanted to replay the fight we'd had on the phone earlier in the week about my leaving for the day. We wouldn't see each other again until the following weekend. I pulled on my winter hiking clothes: Capilene long johns, Gore-tex pants, and a wool shirt. I dressed lightly for snowshoeing, letting the exercise generate most of my warmth. The only drawback was stopping for lunch, when the cold would quickly creep up my spine. I tied my boot laces and strapped on my gaiters.

We'd spent Saturday night in a sweat lodge honoring the dead. A decade earlier, my girlfriend had nearly been killed in a passenger car that hit a tractor-trailer backing up for some reason along the shoulder of the Thruway. She didn't remember the crash. But she did remember walking into the tunnel of white light, an experience she shared with other members of her near-death-experience group that met in the sweat lodge. Our host in the western Catskills had built an igloo-shaped frame with rounded saplings that he'd covered with tarps, carpets, and a bear rug over the door. Once we'd settled inside in the complete darkness, he'd splashed a ladle of water on the fire-heated rocks in the center pit. The steam had ripped through my nose. Uncontrollable sweat slid down my skin. I'd known I had to let go of my ego. Our host had sung an Indian prayer, while my girlfriend had cried. She was back in the white light, trying to reach her friend in the passenger car who'd died.

Two months earlier, my mother had died in her nursing home, after spending ten years in a wheelchair with a mind so scrambled by strokes she couldn't engage in a conversation beyond repeatedly pleading: "I need my food tray." Minutes after finishing dinner, she'd feared she was starving again. One Christmas Eve my father, brother, and I had let her go too far. We'd brought a lemon cake from a bakery, her favorite in the past. She'd devoured her slice. Moments later it had come right back up as lemon soup on her plate. She'd lived in a purgatory of modern medicine that kept her helplessly alive.

The last time I'd seen her was under a white blanket in a cardboard casket printed with wood grain. With one knee raised over the other she'd apparently died trying to roll onto her side to hold the bed's safety railing. Now her face lay upwards with closed eyelids that looked deflated. Brushing aside her short pewter hair, I placed my hand on her forehead to feel a coldness like a cobblestone. My throat ached, choking down sobs, but I wanted to know what death felt like.

Amid all this loss I desperately wanted goals in my life. Here was one: finish climbing the Catskill 3500 peaks in winter. After moving from Manhattan into my Catskills log cabin, I'd hiked the thirty-five summits over 3,500 feet within six months, an accomplishment that made me feel like a genuine resident of these mountains. I'd learned to identify bear claw marks on beech trees, pileated woodpecker holes as large as my face, wild turkey tracks in the snow. And I'd fallen in love with snowshoeing. In some ways winter was my favorite season both at home with a wood stove and in the field amid the quiet solitude and stark black and white beauty. Under bare forests the mountains appeared more rugged and monumental, exposing their cliffs like stone ribs. Climbing them seemed more of an accomplishment. By now, my third year in the Catskills, I needed only five more peaks to earn my Catskill 3500 Club winter patch. But I had only three weekends until spring.

In the kitchen another early-riser offered to make me an omelet, but I didn't want to delay. I filled my canteen with warm water that would cool soon enough. I squeezed the side pockets of my green daypack to be sure they were stuffed with mittens and hat. Ready, I slipped out the door without letting our host's cocker spaniel run loose.

It was the last day of February. Winter looked beaten. The snow had receded up into the hills. This old farmland lay bare with dull green lawn grass and nearby fields of blond plant stalks. Hanging mist revealed the valley but smothered the ridges. As soon as I stepped off the porch, my glasses smeared with droplets. A miserable day for hiking, but I wasn't going back.

In Margaretville I stopped at the gas mart to tank up and buy breakfast to go, along with a chicken-salad sandwich for lunch. Driving off, I sipped weak coffee, smelling gasoline on my fingers, and chewed a plain bagel. The radio forecast drizzle all day.

At the end of Spruceton Road I parked, hoisted my daypack, and started my trek. Maybe this hike wouldn't be the best, but I wasn't here to have fun. I was here to bag a peak that had to be done. My mother had never seemed to finish anything, then strokes had stolen her life for ten years in a nursing home. The bureau in my childhood bedroom had been stuffed with her old clippings and papers. I'd kept one of her "to do" lists that had never been completed: "To get tweezers for facial hairs" checked; "Call Jane and Richard Brooks re: Harvard-Yale Nov 21st football game" not checked. I refused to let my life drift sideways the way hers had.

The first two miles were straightforward, following a snow-shoe-packed trail up to the crest of Diamond Notch, where the bushwhack began. Two years earlier I'd learned this route from a veteran hike leader of the Catskill 3500 Club who'd found the summit canister three times in three attempts, a remarkable record on this featureless ridgeline where another hiker I'd met had gone zero for six. The successful leader hadn't taken our group from the notch straight up to the prow of the ridgeline. That would have forced us to spend lots of time bashing through the dense summit forest of spruce and fir trees, an experience akin to shoving through car wash brushes made of dead branches that poke and whip around your eyes and everyplace else. Bushwhackers joke about self-flagellation, but nobody enjoys this experience. Instead, our guide had set her compass bearing to angle up the side of the long ridgeline, skirting below the conifers for a half a mile before finally climbing onto the ridgetop, where we found the canister in ten minutes, a minor miracle considering that there's no evidence of a summit anywhere in the flat forest until you suddenly come upon the small rise leading up to the canister tree.

Following her approach, I took a bearing: 132° east. In my snowshoes, using hiking poles for balance, I started kicking my way up the steep slope of the lower notch, finding the snow good and solid. Soon I broke a sweat, my jitters subsided. For the first time this morning, I felt glad to be taking this hike. The snowpack looked clean and untouched, a virgin winter unlike the ragged remnants down in the valleys. Behind me the mist curtain hid all but the base of the mountain across the notch. I'd spend my day alone in the belly of the clouds.

Above the lower notch, the slope grew easier. I regularly checked my bearing to avoid the ridge prow, a mistake easy to make if I hiked straight up the mountainside. Instead, I kept to my angle. Softly I sang my favorite hiking song, U2's "Who's Gonna Ride Your Wild Horses." To counter my sweating I unzipped the slats under my jacket's armpits. I appreciated the mist cooling my face. Sooner than expected I saw the jumbled rocky escarpment below the ridgeline plateau, which I kept to my right for a while, not wanting to fight the spruce and fir too soon. Finally, my bearing insisted I ascend to the top. I climbed a gap in the rocks and crawled up into the prickly branch skirt of my first spruce of the day.

After wiggling through this barrier, I found the summit forest to be more forgiving than I remembered. It was easy to dodge between trees. The problem was determining which way the forest floor sloped uphill. It didn't, at least not far in any one direction. Herd paths worn by previous hikers circled among the trees like figure eights or worse. After stepping across the same fat log for the third time, I abandoned the ground approach and studied the gaps in the tree canopy. In the distance stood a tall spruce tree, a sentinel. It must be on the summit mound. But walking closer, I lost track of which tree was tallest. None in the area wore the orange canister anyway. I tried another sentinel, then a third, a fourth. Finally, I stopped for a canteen break. I picked out twigs and needles that had fallen down my neck. According to my watch, I'd spent twenty minutes on this goose chase. My snow-shoe prints diagrammed a Gordian knot in the snow.

In fact, I already stood on the top of Southwest Hunter Moun-tain, didn't I? This summit was a plateau, not a peak. What differ-ence did the canister make? This sport wasn't an Easter egg hunt. Besides, the Catskill 3500 Club didn't check summit registers before admitting members. They took your word for it. Surely, I wouldn't be the first hiker to check off Southwest Hunter with-out technically scribbling my name in the canister notebook. Did they really expect me to spend my afternoon wandering around these stupid trees?

From here I planned to bushwhack across the spur saddle to intercept the Devil's Path trail and hike up Hunter Mountain to the fire tower. If I wanted to finish before dark, I couldn't dawdle. But the hard part of the hike was over. I laid my map flat on the snow and took my bearing across the saddle: 80° east.

Sometimes nothing succeeds like quitting. Ten minutes later I came upon frozen boot tracks in a herd path that took me right up the summit hump, larger than I remembered. Bold as a traffic cone the orange canister was nailed six feet up a spruce tree in a small clearing worn by hikers. I pulled out the ziplock bag that held the registration book and proudly printed my name with the stubby pencil. This hike had turned into a triumph. I'd found the canister all by myself! How many others could say that? Not the hiker who'd gone zero for six.

From here I followed the boot tracks eastwards. The saddle would take half an hour to cross. After a gradual descent the summit conifers gave way to a roomier forest with scattered birches standing over smaller spruce. By paralleling the saddle crest a hundred feet down along the northern side, I crossed through more openings and made great time. Wading through a stand of baby spruce, a Bonsai Christmas tree farm, I lost the boot tracks in the snow, but didn't care. I'd soon intersect the trail. I wondered why these white birches at higher elevations had salmon-pink bark. It was one of those nature mysteries I'd long meant to answer in a field guide but had always forgotten by the time I took my hot shower, sipped a hot chocolate, and checked my messages at home. This time I'd try to remember. It would be fun to learn something new about the woods.

I glanced at my compass, although I didn't need to. The topography was guiding me right across the saddle. The crest had been easy to parallel. In the shifting mist above the birch branches I sensed the massive sweep of Hunter Mountain just ahead like a photograph about to emerge in developing fluid.

But my compass needle pointed backwards. It said I was walking 180° in the wrong direction.

That couldn't be. I'd walked straight through an open forest. If I'd scrambled around rock crevices or ducked under trees, I might have gotten turned around, but I hadn't. I hadn't made any turns at all. Plus I had a great sense of direction. My ex-wife had said so. My girlfriend said so. I knew so. I could emerge from Manhattan subway stops and know which way to turn on the busy streets. I could explore rural roads in the car for hours and

finish where I wanted to be. I'd led friends on Catskill bushwhacks they'd found as disorienting as a circus fun house, but I'd known where we were the whole time.

I shook my compass. Perhaps it had stopped like a dead watch. But the red needle was alive and jiggling. It just wouldn't point the right way.

I opened my map on the snow. I took a fresh bearing, but the needle still aimed the wrong way. I studied the brown contour lines on the map. Southwest Hunter had the shape of a small lima bean that suddenly, sickeningly seemed an absolute lie. This mountain was huge and pitiless now that I felt confused. Without a trail, without a good bearing, I could walk for miles without finding any signs of people. All these pink birch trees that a moment ago I'd found so beautiful with their individual shapes and twists now surrounded me like an anonymous crowd, heartless survivors that didn't care about me. They presided over life and death every day.

What if I was only a few hundred feet from the trail? Certainly, I'd walked far enough across the saddle. Bushwhacking, you often didn't see a trail until you're ten feet away. In minutes I could be standing on the well-trampled Devil's Path, chuckling about this silly panic. The Devil's Acre lean-to would be nearby. Last fall I'd spent a wonderful hour there with my friends, Quincy and Tim, from the City, who'd taken a weekday break from their wives and work to join me for a trail hike that had the spirit of a Boy Scout

Old Timer's Day. For an hour, we'd tried without success to ignite the charred logs in the lean-to's fire ring, and we'd shared funny stories. Both in their early fifties they were my older, brotherly mentors. Tim had been one of the first to encourage my poetry. Quincy had recently visited Hollywood to sell an option to one of his plays. But where were they now? Where was the lean-to? The trail? Where was I?

I was standing in the cold mist staring at the cruelty of birch trees. Could I have chosen worse weather? In snow I could stay relatively dry, but in this mist everything got wet, threatening my body heat. People suffered hypothermia at forty degrees, not twenty degrees. So long as I kept moving, I'd stay warm, but where was I going? What if I spent the night? Some day hikers carried emergency supplies: a sleeping bag, a bivouac sack, a fistful of Power Bars. All excellent ideas. I hadn't even bothered to pack a second sandwich.

What an idiot.

In the next clearing I spotted a pink ribbon of survey tape tied on a spruce branch. Thank God! Someone had been here. Maybe they'd marked their own route from the trail to Southwest Hunter, cheating in what should be wilderness, but a lifeline for me. I ran ahead, lumbering on my snowshoes as my daypack bounced on my back. I felt damned lucky. These silly pink tags would save me. But after fifty feet the row of ribbons stopped. How could that be? Nobody left ribbons in the middle of nowhere. But I couldn't panic. I had to be systematic. At the last ribbon I walked fifty feet in three directions. Then a hundred feet. Two hundred feet.

Now I couldn't even find the ribbons again. Every one of these small openings looked the same. Twisted birches and sullen spruce. I threw my daypack on the snow.

All alone.

Maybe I deserved it.

Who cared anyway? My father? He hadn't called in a month. My girlfriend? She just wanted to get married. My mother? I'd hated visiting her in the nursing home, an institution of zombies. She'd never even understood that I lived in a cabin. To her, I'd been permanently twenty-three and married, for some reason, to my cousin, Muggsie. My father kept having to reassure her that it was okay to pee in her diaper. For ten years, she hadn't understood anything I'd tried to tell her. I could have climbed a hundred mountains and she wouldn't have known.

How I hated this shifting mist, always about to reveal something it never did.

I needed to stay warm. In my daypack was an extra sweater and mittens, my sandwich, and a canteen three-quarters full. In the bottom was an emergency first aid kit I hadn't checked in three years. Surely it had matches. Maybe a space blanket. Probably medicines that were expired.

I couldn't think about getting injured. Not here. Not now. Not my foot turned sideways like the time I was a tackling dummy in eighth-grade football practice. On the hospital bed before surgery I rolled my knee back and forth and watched my numb rubbery foot lie motionless against a triangular white prop. No connection. My mother almost fainted when she walked into the room. But she was dead. And I was lost.

"Hello!" I shouted. "Anybody?"

I thought I heard something. I waited. And waited. The dead silence of winter. The occasional pattering of wet snow slipping off trees. Had I heard only an echo?

"Fuck you!"

*Stop it!* I thought. *You're panicking.* I opened my map on the snow.

Maybe I should simply plunge down into the valley. It was guaranteed to lead down to a stream which was guaranteed to flow down to a road. The Catskills weren't so big that you couldn't reach humanity in a day. By nightfall I'd be soggy and sore, but I'd be knocking on somebody's door, sheepishly asking for a ride around the mountain back to my car.

At the top of the rock bluff the spruce grew thick as a hedge. I barged through the rough branches, then settled on my butt and slid off the edge seven feet down into a snow embankment. Standing up from my sloppy landing, I shook the snow out of my sleeves and brushed it off the folds in my jacket. The first step was always a doozy. Hadn't somebody said that on the moon? I readjusted my daypack, which had nearly gotten snagged up in the trees. I checked that my compass still hung from its cord around my neck.

On the bluff behind me I noticed a green band of frosted moss. A streak of dirt. Around me the snow was much thinner, even bare in spots. A fallen tree trunk lay glistening wet, not sleeved with snow. I was standing on a southern exposure. Yet hadn't I just dropped off the northern side of the saddle? I looked at my compass. The red needle pointed uphill at north. Downhill was south. The melted snow told me the same. The compass was right. It was my instincts that were trying to kill me.

I felt relieved. I didn't need to understand what had gone wrong. I needed to trust my compass and get out of here. To hell with the lean-to, Hunter Mountain, or anyplace else. I'd head back to Diamond Notch where I started.

Rock climbing in snowshoes may be a clumsy art, but I managed to hoist myself back up into the hedge of spruces, then crawl through branches into the small clearing. I smiled at what I saw: a yellow pee hole, my snowshoe prints pacing in all directions as if an entire patrol had argued here. The record of my fear. I laid my map on the snow and took a bearing: 290° west. This time while walking, I raised my compass every few moments like a prayer book. I knew better than to trust my line of sight.

For an hour, I didn't recognize any of the trees or topography, but I remained confident of my course along the northern side of Southwest Hunter Mountain. High to my left ran the balcony of jumbled cliff rocks and dense conifers on the ridge plateau. Down here the snow lay soft and deep, a challenge for snowshoeing.

Walking felt like shoveling with my feet. But I was glad to trade this labor in return for knowing where I was going.

At a flattop boulder I stopped for lunch. During my half hour of fear, I hadn't even sipped from my canteen. After swiping snow off the rock, I hoisted up my butt and slung off my daypack. The nylon had grown stiff icy skin in the freezing drizzle. After shaking looseness back into the pack, I tried the zipper. It, too, had frozen. Jesus Christ! I could be lost and not even able to reach my food! Then the zipper gave. I took a deep breath. I wasn't lost anymore. I had to believe that.

The water was delicious. But I gave up on the sandwich after three bites. It tasted fine, but I had no appetite. And the boulder under my butt was cold. It reminded me too much of the cobblestone of my dead mother's forehead. I hopped off and started marching: 290° west with each and every step. Then I spotted my morning snowshoe tracks ascending the steep hillside. I'd made it! I started bounding down between the trees, my churning feet trampolining through the deep powder on my springy snowshoes. I was nearly skiing, sort of running, almost tumbling. I was laughing and loving this crazy descent through the merciful snow, my private playground in the wild.

# Seeing the Forest for the Trees

Michael Perkins

THE DEVIL'S PATH is an aptly named hiking trail that runs westward from Overlook Mountain to Hunter Mountain and beyond. Years ago, when I was stronger and more foolhardy, I trekked over this range of six peaks in four days and three nights.

Looking back on that insane feat, I think that my boots must not have touched the ground. Certainly I didn't have time to see very much, except for the next trail marker. I passed through first-growth forest on Indian Head, Twin and, Plateau Mountains. I passed unusual land forms—landslides and talus slopes, kettles in glacial till. I blundered through old burns and trudged up bark roads, oblivious to the history of the landscape I whizzed through. I was like a clueless tourist on Tinker Street in Woodstock, who strolls blindly past layers of architectural history, wondering what all the fuss associated with Woodstock is about, deaf to the ghosts who call out to him.

Many hikers are like that younger self, tourists in the landscape, racing to bag mountain peaks. Today, given the leisure, I would devote two weeks to the same hike. I wouldn't miss the trees for the forest. I'd stop and stare.

I would also have memorized the relevant sections of Michael Kudish's essential *The Catskill Forest: A History*, so I'd know what I was looking at. At home, I would consult it as frequently as I do Spider and Anita Barbour's *Wild Flora of the Northeast* or Alf Evers's tomes on the human history of our area. I would only regret that a large hardcover book weighing more than two pounds is no *vade mecum* for an aging long-distance hiker.

Although what you see along the way is more important than getting to the summit, if you've been to enough mountaintops, you're permanently changed.

Dr. Kudish, a professor of forestry at Paul Smith's College, has been studying the Catskill forest for over thirty years, and he has come to view our region from a mountaintop perspective, as he tells us in his introduction:

"Most people view the Catskills from the valleys up, with the ridgetops distant, perhaps unreachable, foreign, mysterious, foreboding or even threatening. I view the Catskills from the summits down, observing people swarming up the valleys, chaotically creating disturbances at the lowest elevation to the greatest degree and at the highest elevations to the least degree... To me, the summits are the norm, the comprehensible, the familiar, the simple. The valleys are foreign, mysterious, complex, threatening and confounding."

This is about as personal as Kudish gets in *The Catskill Forest*, but it seasons the dry, plain style he employs to describe the wonders he has seen and researched. Reading him, I imagined how Thoreau, with his naturalist's lust for fact and measurement and exactitude, would have loved consulting Kudish before his own hiking trip in the Catskills in 1844.

Kudish's theme is how the forest has changed over time. Until 1994, he believed that its development could only be traced back four hundred years, but his ambition was to look back to the period of deglaciation fourteen thousand years ago. Radiocarbon dating and new techniques for sampling bog peat for plant fossils have now enabled him to look back into time more than thirteen thousand years.

He has divided the results of his studies into five sections, leading off with the story of how a forest grows. The impact of humans on its development is scrutinized, from Native Americans to bluestone quarrying, and the history of land acquisitions and the forest preserve, reforestation, recreation and fires is laid out in detail.

For armchair naturalists and those concerned with the pressures of development, all of this material is a necessary resource. For hikers, Kudish's section on the mountain ranges provides very specific information and many surprises. Picking almost at random from this treasure trove, but staying close to home, I plucked these nuggets of information, each one sufficient to start a reverie or inspire a desire to go out and look for myself at some previously overlooked feature of the landscape.

The three-toothed cinquefoil, a species of arctic vegetation, may be found at an elevation of 3,000 to 3,025 feet on Overlook Mountain. The significance of this is that the Catskills are too low to possess alpine zones, yet up there on a ledge is a site, under an acre in size, which Kudish tells us has never been forested since deglaciation. This means that a climb up Overlook can take the hiker back in time to just after the age of the glaciers, when ice covered our area. (The parent material of Catskill soil is glacial till, which covers ninety percent of the region.)

The great Mohawk chief Joseph Brant fought on the British side in the Catskills during the Revolutionary War. I've always wondered where his camp was. Kudish locates it "below the col between the High Peak and Roundtop at 2,540 feet." I'm already planning the hike I'll make to find it.

Three areas of kettles in glacial till, "remarkable and rare landforms in the Catskills," occur near Woodstock. One is in the Mink Hollow col at the base of Plateau Mountain; it's one of the sights I missed during my marathon hike.

In Kudish's book, I learned for the first time about the danger to the forest that is threatened by the woolly adelgid killing hemlock trees; the damage perpetrated by the gypsy moth on Ticeteneyck and Tonshi mountains in 1989; that Native Americans, who burned the forests regularly every fall, had fifteen-acre cornfields stretching from Kingston to Olive; the location of bluestone quarries and tanneries; all about soils, climate, trees; the distinction between first-growth and old-growth forest; the myth of the hemlock-covered mountains—but I'll stop. Kudish's chest of riches is wide and deep. His extensive notes, bibliography and index are a pleasure to peruse. A separate, beautiful and useful color map (yes, suitable for framing) augments the many maps, tables and illustrations in the book.

Michael Kudish's *The Catskill Forest: A History* is both fascinating and indispensable, a marvelous lens which helps us to see clearly what we are looking at—and, by so doing, deepens our sense of place.

# Circumnavigation@3500

Will Nixon

THE GREAT QUESTION comes after climbing all thirty-five of the Catskill 3500 Club peaks for an honorary green patch, then climbing them again in winter for a blue patch: what next for the goal obsessed? My girlfriend suggested having sex on each summit, but we broke up before getting started. My older hiking buddy, Paul Levine, scaled down to 3400 foot peaks, then 3300 foot peaks. Now he's ambling toward the Catskills hundred highest, finding mountains I'd never heard of like Cave and West Cave and Old Clump. (Actually, Paul didn't finish the 3500 foot peaks until his sixties, so he's really picked up his pace.) Another friend, Roger Wall, went south to take up rock climbing in the Shawangunks, a sport I tried twice before accepting that I was about as agile as lichen on rock.

Then Roger came back with an idea: let's circumnavigate Slide Mountain at 3500 feet. Rather than conquering the Catskills' highest peak by marching to the top, we'd embrace its wildness by bushwhacking its girth. It turned out that Roger, who divides his life between a house in Pine Hill and an apartment in Tribeca, had spent some urban hours studying contour maps with a magnifying glass, trying to imagine what these remote places really looked like. As he later wrote about our trip, "I like to think that when Magellan, the most famous circumnavigator, sailed around the world, he proved more than the Earth was not flat. Perhaps he gave us another way, more intimate and indirect, of experiencing landscape." I knew what Roger meant. On trail hikes my mind easily slips into distracted thoughts that I chew on like gum. Bushwhacking forces me to pay attention to the terrain. Letting trails do the directing takes some of the wilderness out of the experience.

By way of the jeep road trail from Route 47, Slide Mountain is one of the High Peak's easier climbs, a steady three-mile ascent.

On our way up, Roger and I talked about all kinds of things: marriage, divorce, Captain Beefheart, the musician. We'd chosen a sunny day in April before the trees unfurled their leaves to hide the views. The waxy green and maroon mottled trout lily blades of early spring had knifed through the ground mat of brown leaves, but their delicate nodding yellow flowers hadn't yet appeared. We were at the cusp of the season, though the temperature was climbing toward summer.

At the 3500 feet sign on the jeep trail Roger set his altimeter. Now the much harder hike began. Measured by string, the 3500 contour line on the map was eight miles long. It made a disfigured starfish shape with short and long legs curving westwards, plus the fat leg east that was the saddle to Cornell Mountain. What worried us was the northeastern bowl on Slide where contour lines nearly merged into solid brown steepness.

On the trail from Slide to Cornell the descent gets so severe in places that one rock face has a long wooden ladder. If Roger and I encountered terrain like that we'd be in trouble. But we wouldn't know until we got there.

We stepped off the jeep road into the beech forest, spotting an old fire ring, evidence people had heeded the warning sign not to camp above 3500 feet between March Twenty-First and December Twenty-First. Beyond that lay open woods without paths. This western ridge is rather gentle, so we found easy walking through leaves and over an occasional fallen log. The trees weren't large, save for a massive yellow birch with its grandfatherly bark cracked and flaky, almost like an old maple's. I wondered how long it had stood here unseen by anyone.

Soon enough, we came to a herd path, a discernible trail but little used. On the hiking map it's a dotted black line on private land owned by the Winnisook Club down on Route 47. Yet for decades in the nineteenth century this route was the trail up Slide. As described by Alf Evers in *The Catskills: From Wilderness to Woodstock*, this path was created and maintained by a local man named Jim Dutcher soon after the surveyor Arnold Guyot surprised everyone by declaring Slide the highest mountain in the Catskills in 1872. (The hoteliers near Kaaterskill High Peak on the eastern escarpment overlooking the Hudson refused at first to believe that they no longer had the highest mountain in the Catskills.) To make the climb up Slide easier for women in dresses, Dutcher laid down stone steps. In my years of hiking the Catskills, I've only seen one woman in a dress, a teenager from the Bruderhof Community at the top of Platte Clove. She was also in bare feet.

In 1886, a state forest commissioner, Christopher Cox, led a party of prominent politicians to the summit to mark the newly established Catskill Forest Preserve. "The Dutcher trail was in deplorable condition," Evers wrote. "The erosion caused by spring rains and melting snow had not been repaired, trees felled across the trail by a recent storm had not been removed, and it required twice the usual hour and a half for the commissioner and his party to make the climb." The problem was that Cox and his crowd, all Democrats, had snubbed Dutcher, a Republican, to hire a Democrat as their guide. More than a century later, our political parties haven't gotten any friendlier, but at least we're not fighting it out on the trails.

Up on a nearby bench in the slope, Roger and I found a boggy clearing of brown grass hummocks and green sphagnum moss, an enchanting surprise. Maybe it was the spot Evers described where Commissioner Cox had picked up a handful of moss and, "as he squeezed water from it, explained that this was a good example of the usefulness to man of forests such as that covering most of Slide—their spongy floors held water and released it slowly to replenish rivers and check floods." It was small bogs like this one, not the spectacular scenery, that led our forefathers to protect the Catskills as a watershed, not as a peak baggers' playground for the likes of Roger and me. Whatever the history, we remained grateful for this wilderness three hours drive from Manhattan.

By contouring at 3500 feet, we were doing ourselves one great favor; we were skirting the balsam fir forest higher up the mountain, where the bushwhacking would be fierce. Still, we had to wrestle with hobblebushes if we couldn't find animal paths. These woody shrubs, a member of the viburnum family, may not be as dense as mountain laurels, but they're no fun. "Aptly named," Roger wrote later of hobblebushes. He wondered if their roots might be connected, sending signals ahead to entangle us as we tried to progress. Yet Roger and I actually shared a fondness for hobblebushes, a plant that signifies the Catskill High Peaks to me, since I've never seen them in the valleys below. In a poem I've described their showy May flowers as "white saucers serving the fragrance of earth." Roger, a gardener, has planted one in his lawn in Pine Hill. It looks scraggly and forlorn amid the groomed grass, but it's surviving.

Across the valley, we saw Slide's northern spur, a ridgeline more than a mile long rising to 3,640 feet at the far end. At first Roger mistook it for a separate mountain until we saw the land bridge to Slide. I, myself, was amazed to discover such a significant peak that I hadn't know about until now. On the map it didn't even have a name. Without Slide stealing the glory, it would have been the Catskills' twenty-fourth tallest summit. Later, Michael Kudish, the forest historian, told me that it did have a name back in the nineteenth century: Schekelmoose. And what was a Schekelmoose? Mike didn't know.

Had we been purists, Roger and I would have followed the 3500-foot contour around this spur rather than shortcutting over the top. We weren't purists. We hiked up through a sunny clearing of brown ferns flattened by winter and entered among scattered firs. The moment of truth had come, the drop-off into the northeastern bowl. Would we find cliffs like ruined castle walls too steep to descend? To our relief, we looked down into a forested hillside, steep but anchored with grand white birches. We wondered if anyone had been here before, if we represented the arrival of the white man in this magnificent forest. Such a scenario seemed implausible, yet we relished the feeling of discovery. After all, how many people would be nutty enough to circumnavigate Slide Mountain?

Awkwardly, we got down from the ridgeline's cliffy rim onto the northeastern slope, which was steep but passable. ("Awkwardly" is a euphemism for sliding my butt down a bushy gully, then pausing at the bottom to untangle the compass string almost strangling my neck.) We traversed slowly but safely, alternating between bushy thickets and jumbled slabs of moss-covered rocks. That so many large rocks were so loose surprised me. Thousands of years after the Ice Age, this mountainside still hadn't settled into place. I stepped quickly the moment tippy stones began scraping under my feet. But I paused in secure spots to marvel at this moss garden, a combination of miniature fern-like leaves, pool table velvet, and pincushion plants that I could sink my finger into for an inch. Roger had been right about traversing. On a regular hike I never would have found myself playing with moss.

Cornell and Wittenberg Mountains loomed across from our bowl, a much closer and more intimate view of them than the one I knew from Giant Ledge, a lookout two miles north of this spot. We were in the lap of Slide Mountain well up from Woodland Valley and well down from the conifer rim against the blue sky. We felt exposed yet protected, small humans welcomed in a Catskills much bigger than they looked from trails.

We came to a series of three cascading brooks, mossy staircases with steps and pools down an otherwise dull brown mountainside. "Red faced and sweating, I splashed water on my face and neck," Roger wrote. "Will filled his empty water bottle from the rushing water, then threw caution to the wind and drank unfiltered water from the source. I felt like we were in an emerald paradise."

By lunchtime we reached the Cornell saddle. "The trail, a narrow single lane, rises out of the forest like a superhighway,"

Roger wrote. "I feel as though I've reentered civilization." I shared the feeling. We considered taking the trail over the summit and down to our cars. After all, we'd done the hard part, hadn't we? But we resisted. After lunch we continued on the southeastern side of Slide, a gentle slope filled with beech trees, but also a bare forest shadeless against the unseasonably hot sun.

At last we made a hard right turn into the upper valley of Deer Shanty Brook. Before thinking better, we pushed our way into dense firs. Unlike the spindly summit conifers under which you duck and bash your way through a thousand twiggy branches, these were large trees slapping us around with branch boughs. In one jam I had to straddle a fallen trunk high enough that my boots dangling in the air above thick branches. What if these branches weren't close to the ground? What if they were a trap door above an open gap in rocks? Fortunately, I landed solidly. But I didn't like this green-needled jungle gym one bit.

"Do you think it would be easier higher up?" asked Roger, trailing behind me so as not to get slapped by my branches.

"I don't know," I said.

"Do you think we have much farther to the stream?"

"I don't know."

"You're not supposed to say that."

A grimness had set in. These trees were a punishment we didn't deserve, not at the end of a long hot day. We had no choice but to thrash forward. Loose needles stuck to the back of my sweaty neck. Then, suddenly, we shoved through a branch bough and saw the brook with an open forest on the other hillside. (The next day my Pilates teacher would see my scratched arms and say, "You've been hiking.") Roger celebrated by filling his hat with water and dousing his head. I filled my canteen for the fourth time that day and decided that this was one of the best Catskills hikes I'd ever taken.

The final traverse across a small valley to the jeep trail looked short on the map but took forever on foot. Roger's knees ached, as did an ankle from a winter sprain. I was just whipped. The back of my blue shirt, Roger told me, displayed white clouds from my sweat. I found my odd souvenir for the day, an orange "No Trespassing" sign from the Winnisook Club dragged half a mile from their boundary by a porcupine, judging by the teeth-polished metal where the animal had scraped paint. But I was too tired to stuff the sign in my daypack. I tossed it back to the ground for another bushwhacker to find in a decade or two.

At last we stepped across stones bordering the jeep trail onto well trodden ground a few yards from the 3500 foot elevation sign. We were amazed by our luck at returning to our starting point, especially since Roger's altimeter now read 3590.

At 5:30 we reached the parking lot, where we'd started at seven that morning. We soaked our feet in the cold stream and knew we'd done something special. Roger later wrote, "Moving slowly around the mountain, pushing against fir boughs, touching rock, hearing the rush of brooks let us share the deep secrets of the landscape together." I agreed. I'd climbed Slide many times on the jeep trail, but until now I hadn't known how big and wild this mountain really was. You can't hug a mountain the way you can hug a friend, but we'd come close. In the trail register I checked us out. Three others had signed in that day. But under "Destination" only Roger had written "circumnavigation@3500." Who knew if anyone had done it before? Who knew if anyone would do it again?

# A Night on Mink Hollow with Porky

Michael Perkins

A FEW TIMES A YEAR when I was in my forties and fifties I climbed into the blue mountains to spend a night or two camping out. After hiking all day on steep Catskill trails I sought out a flat place with a view and settled in for the night. I traveled light, no fires, my only shelter a plastic sheet and a sleeping bag. But one October when I was on a five-day trek on the Devil's Path, climbing up and down from Overlook Mountain to Hunter Mountain, I stopped at a wooden shelter at the top of Mink Hollow. Luxury, for a change, I thought. I ate my dinner of sardines and sourdough bread with relish, and sipped brandy as I watched the blue hour fade to black. When I crawled into my bag I anticipated blissful slumber. I thought of the hard logs under me as the arms of Morpheus.

But sleep was not to come. The host of my wilderness guesthouse announced himself with greedy braying and pitiful whining. I stuck my head out of my sleeping bag and saw a large silverback porcupine staring longingly up at the pack I'd hung on the shelter wall. I tossed some rocks in his direction and closed my eyes. The moon rose and bathed the open-faced shelter in silvery light. The wind picked up and the trees shook; Porky scrunched leaves and woke me again and again. One of the rocks hit him and he lumbered off, shaking his quills in frustration. Mexican standoff.

I stand well over six feet, and hold a valid membership in a ferocious species. Porky's a member of the order Rodentia. He can grow to be thirty inches long—with a seven-inch tail attached—and weighs about thirty pounds, when he's getting his ration of bark. Sure, he's a big boy, but he's slow and stupid, a boon to hungry people because he's easily killed. He lives by girdling trees and chewing wooden structures, like wilderness shelters and outhouses. A prickly schmoo.

Nevertheless, if you're on top of a mountain solo after dark and it's you in your underwear versus a determined rodent who eats outhouses, even the strongest soul might experience a moment or two of primal fear. While you're fending off Porky's onslaught—he can smell the sardine oil!—and tossing and turning, it is natural to contemplate the etiology of fear.

On a hiking trip I could, after all, have a heart attack, appendicitis, or snake bite; I could fall and break bones, I could get lost, succumb to hypothermia—or a crazy person might happen along, looking for a *Deliverance* experience.

Then there are bears, lynx, cougar, rabid raccoons, skunks, bats, coyotes, hooting owls and buzzing skeeters.

And Porky.

What better place than a ramshackle inn on top of a mountain in the middle of the night to take stock of one's courage? I lay awake making a balance sheet of bravery and timidity. I recalled that Indian boys long ago had been sent on vision quests, which usually involved spending time alone on mountaintops. I thought of primitive ancestors waiting for dawn and the return of the sun. I realized that Porky was teaching me some home truths, and that the proper attitude was gratitude. I saw what I had to do. I pried open a tin of sardines and placed it on the ground with a respectful bow.

I slept the sleep of the brave the rest of the night through.

||||||||||||||||||||||||||||||||||||||||||||||||||||||||||||||||||||||||||||||||||||||||||||||||

I'll admit that my beloved Overlook Mountain can be a pedestrian highway. For a respite I hike the Mink Hollow Trail from the end of Mink Hollow Road three miles up to the notch between Plateau and Sugarloaf Mountains. Hikers usually continue up these steeply sided peaks for a full day of climbing, but I turn around for a shorter afternoon walk. This route has no views, but it envelops me in the forest, which has a stream in the lower reaches. This trail also has quite a history as a road. As Alf Evers reported in *Woodstock: History of an American Town*, settlers opened this route before the American Revolution. In 1783 some sixty men built it into a connector to the Schoharie Creek Valley. "Very soon the route became alive with workers with axes, picks and shovels," Evers wrote. "Whites and blacks, free men and slaves toiled together as the road moved upward from Lake Hill and then down to the banks of the Schoharie Kill." Through the nineteenth century this road had a good run. By the age of the automobile its time had past. Today, the abandoned route has eroded so badly in places that loose rocks make it an ankle twister. I love it anyway. For years, my favorite outhouse in the Catskills served the lean-to in the notch. Notorious for their salt cravings, porcupines chew almost anything with sodium, including wood, paint, etc. I opened the outhouse door to discover that the wooden seat box was gone. The toilet seat ring floated in midair like a halo. A shrine, I suppose, to Porky's unquenchable appetite. –W.N.
||||||||||||||||||||||||||||||||||||||||||||||||||||||||||||||||||||||||||||||||||||||||||||||||

# The King of the Trailhead Parking Lot

Will Nixon

*The Hiker*

Is it true that porcupines will eat
your brake lines for the salt?
I see one now in the parking lot,
waddling in a suspicious direction,
as if he thinks my car is his breakfast.
The bum. I came here for the birds
like the yellow bellied sapsucker
I just saw drumming the aluminum gutter
of an abandoned cottage. A male.
A positive identification.
A red, white, and black mask
like a comic book superhero,
a spectacular start to my day,
and now, now this god damned porcupine
lugging his loose backload of quills
...wait until I find a rock.


*The Porcupine*

The nervous ape: he thinks I'm going to eat
his brake lines, and maybe he's right,
but I wish he could do better
than a Japanese import.
These hikers have gotten so cheap,
I can't remember my last Cadillac.
I've had to turn to trail signs, outhouses,
hiking boots left out for the night,

which don't taste as good as you might think.
Now the daredevil throws his only rock
wildly in the dirt, as if he doesn't know
I can smell his fear under his morning deodorant.
Well, let me flare my quills a little,
that's all he sees in me anyway,
as if I have no brains, no taste,
no talent for climbing trees to the outer limits
for the choicest leaves.
The hairless beast has no respect,
but at least he didn't bring
one of those god damned dogs.

# My David Complex

Will Nixon

EVERY WEEK *Woodstock Times* readers turn to the letters pages to be amused and appalled. Not by the courtesy notes thanking volunteers for making an event a rousing success. But by the ranters and ravers, the cranks, the blowhards who overwhelm the paper's stated policy against "Ad Hominem attacks, gratuitous name-calling, and threats" with venomous insults and nasty asides. It's awful what some folks write. And such fun to read. I like to believe that I'm above such vitriol—then I fire off a letter myself.

At a Kingston press conference in September 2007 Governor Spitzer announced a grand compromise between environmentalists, the governor's staff, and the developer of a proposed golf resort complex straddling Belleayre Mountain that had embroiled the Catskills in controversy for a decade. (Early on, I'd bushwhacked to the ridgetop slated for golf greens and nabbed an orange survey stake tag as my badge of opposition.) The next morning *The New York Times* editorial page praised the agreement as "a milestone for conservation, for watershed protection and for smart growth in the Catskills." A win-win, to pile on buzz words. Good for the environment. Good for development. I was infuriated.

Ignoring the "no more than 300 words" policy, my letter filled eighteen column inches with my dissection of the deal. There was good news: the ridgetop chosen for a golf course and luxury hotel would now be left "Forever Wild" as part of the Catskill Forest Preserve. Rather than sprawling across the eastern and western ridges of the mountain, the proposed resort would be contained to the western side. The bad news: it was still huge, a faux-Bavarian vacationland village with two hotels, five restaurants, ten retail shops, a golf course, and spas; in sum, the largest hamlet for forty miles around. The crowning outrage was a cul-de-sac for nineteen houses to be built at 3,000 feet, only four hundred feet below the summit, a high-elevation invasion of the Catskills, which, for more than a century, has preserved its mountain ridges. To appreciate this success, you need only stand on the Overlook Mountain summit at dusk to watch the lights twinkle on in the darkening forest of Woodstock and the Hudson Valley. The malls north of Kingston glow like an electronic circuit board. But the great sweep of the Catskills to the west and the north turns pitch black, save for a solitary kickstand of lights down the Belleayre ski slopes. Such a wilderness of darkness is a lot harder to find in our age than a developer's bedazzlement of lights.

In my letter I didn't direct my ire at Governor Spitzer (remember him?) or the developer (the perennial villain) but at the Catskill Center, a representative of the environmentalists. As a member, I'd received a letter from Tom Alworth, their executive director, touting the compromise as a "great victory!" "'A great victory!'" I shot back in my letter to the editor, "except for the people who live here."

What did I get for my troubles? A lunch invitation from Tom Alworth. By the time we met four months later at Oriole 9 in Woodstock, the grand compromise had basically blown up. Though still legally binding upon the Catskill Center and other groups that signed the agreement, the deal had inspired a fresh crusade by local environmentalists who'd filled public meetings and letters pages with opposition to the proposed mega-resort. Tom Alworth had taken heat not only from me but from people who counted, including one of the Catskill Center's founders. Yet over lunch he couldn't have been friendlier. The "great victory!" tone of his letter was replaced in conversation by conflicted feelings. He, too, hated the idea of nineteen houses at 3,000 feet. But, taken as a whole, he and other negotiators, who were veteran environmental lawyers, believed that they'd gotten the best deal they could. To reject it in favor of going to court was to risk losing more in a judge's decision than they'd won at the negotiating table. Plus, they'd spent a fortune in legal expenses. Why spend more to possibly get less? I sensed that he accepted the agreement not as a triumph but as the harsh reality of what could and could not be accomplished under our legal system.

I was too stubborn to accept the agreement as a good thing. But I respected Tom Alworth's efforts and his willingness to explain matters to me. Plus, I liked him. Earlier in his life he'd written poetry, always a sign of good character. He also had the charisma of a countrified Richard Gere with his high flock of gray hair and his relaxed made-for-the-cameras smile. Years earlier I'd heard him lecture about John Burroughs, the nineteenth century Catskills nature writer, so I knew of his deep love for the woods. Over lunch he was engaging, easy to talk to, accepting of my stubbornness. We listened to smooth jazz background music and enjoyed the chic ambiance of the restaurant, which had artworks hung on the squash-orange walls. The Catskills can seem like a hardscrabble region with limited opportunities and cheap pizzerias. Tom Alworth lent them panache. Then he gave me a lead.

He explained that the agreement included a restriction that those nineteen houses not be visible from state wilderness lands. That's a little more complicated than it sounds. Though the Catskill Forest Preserve is "Forever Wild," the state has segmented these lands into "Wild Forest" and "Wilderness Areas" for management purposes. During negotiations, the environmentalists had sought to make those houses hidden from all state lands, but the developer prevailed by limiting the restriction to "Wilderness Area." No fool, that developer. Most state land in the Belleayre area is "Wild Forest." But, back home after lunch, I spread out my hiking map and discovered that due south of the proposed housing site stood a small peak that I'd never noticed before: Hiram's Knob. Smack dab in a "Wilderness Area." What luck! Tom Alworth had given me the stone for my slingshot. Like David I'd drop Goliath. If the view from Hiram's Knob across a valley to the 3,000- foot elevation was as good as suggested by the map, I'd recruit a photographer to join me there to take a damning picture of the future housing site. We'd kill that cul-de-sac yet.

Paul Levine, my monthly hiking partner from Connecticut, was game. Not that he gave credence to my fantasy of stopping a multi-million dollar development by taking a bushwhack. A business consultant who has worked on everything from tropical sawmills to resort communities to Yankee Stadium during his career, he knows how the world works. But having hiked in the Catskills for fifty years, he's eager to try anything new that we find on a map. So on a clear March morning we started at the Ryder Hollow trailhead between Belleayre and Hiram's Knob. We'd trail hike up to Haynes Mountain then return on a ridgetop bushwhack to Hiram's Knob. As luck would have it, a cell tower at 3,000 feet on Belleayre marked the proposed housing site. If we saw that tower glinting in the sunlight, I'd be a happy warrior: David, indeed.

This morning we had ideal conditions, a shallow blanket of snow that caught sparkles of sunlight through the bare forest. We didn't need snowshoes or crampons. We hiked in boots. ("Bare booting" is the term used by winter hikers.) For the first half mile the trail followed alongside flat streams until it reached a lean-to. One of the mysteries of the Catskills is why some lean-tos are where they are, such as this one fifteen minutes from the parking lot. Of course, you might not find this question very compelling, but it was an observation that launched Paul and me into one of our hiking conversations. You might call what we did philosophizing. Or you might call it silliness. (We once debated for ten minutes whether or not I, having picked up a faded white beer can among the trees and then tossing it a few minutes later was now responsible for littering.) But we enjoyed ourselves. Hiking not only limbers up the body; it loosens up the mind. Reasoning, a practical tool at home and work, becomes playful in the woods with nothing to do but walk and think for six hours of uninterrupted time. Paul and I have debated the nature of love, the meaning of intelligence, the essence of trash. (I still say that I wasn't littering if I merely moved a previously littered can a few hundred feet.)

The one subject Paul and I hadn't debated was the proposed Belleayre resort. From the start, I considered this grand scheme to build mountaintop golf courses, hotels, and a dozen other things in a *nouveau riche* tourist village to be a travesty. To me, the Catskills are the Catskill Forest Preserve, an inspired blending of "Forever Wild" lands at higher elevations and valley communities that change over time but cherish their beautiful surroundings. In his book, *Hope, Human & Wild*, Bill McKibben has argued that the Adirondack Forest Preserve, our giant companion to the north, offers a model to the world in which people must learn how to live among wild areas rather than destroy them. Much as Adirondack conservationists have battled against one outlandish development proposal after another over the decades, we in the Catskills faced our greatest threat from this planned hotel fantasyland. The cynics among us even believed that the project would morph into a casino before it was completed.

In short, this wasn't a topic that lent itself to lighthearted philosophizing. But that's not to say that Paul and I had avoided it completely. One summer day we planned an ambitious bushwhack with two friends that would start up Romer Mountain in Phoenicia, an old ski center now gone to meadow, then ascend Mount Pleasant and finally drop down to Route 28 near the Emerson hotel and restaurant complex. In the morning, turning off Route 28 to leave one car at the finish, we passed the charred yellow hulk of the Emerson hotel that had recently burned. "How'd you like to make a quick $50,000?" I asked Paul. He shot me a look, as in, "This better be good." Dean Gitter, the Emerson's owner and the Belleayre resort developer, had offered a $50,000 reward for the arsonist, a premature offer, it seemed, since it wasn't clear that arson had caused the fire. Cynics saw this headline-grabbing gesture as a smear against resort opponents by implying that one of his enemies had lit the match. By the time I explained this background to Paul, whatever humor my quip might have contained lay dead on the car seat. No matter. I can always come up with another wisecrack. Meanwhile, we pulled up to a white clapboard building, a modest former hotel or rooming house that I recognized as Dean Gitter's offices. After knocking on the door, I met the most gracious of men, a manager who welcomed us to park our car in their lot for the day.

That turned out to be a hell of bushwhack. Not just the usual assortment of brambles and bushes but stringy ground vines that kept tripping us, as if we were walking upon a net cast over ground rocks and logs. Every so often one of us wondered aloud why we hadn't saved this hike for autumn after the leaves had fallen, enabling us to see what surely would be magnificent views. But not that day. Not even from the Mount Pleasant summit, a flat nondescript forest. I set my compass bearing for Route 28, plunging us down the rugged hillside. More than an hour later, to my delight after wandering this way and that through featureless woods, we stepped onto a road less than fifty yards from the car, a navigational bull's-eye. As we changed out of our sweaty shirts, who should emerge from the building but Dean Gitter himself, a chesty man with a smooth gray pony tail and the proud bearing of a country squire. We exchanged friendly greetings. He seemed surprised, possibly impressed that the four of us had spent a hot sticky day thrashing through the woods for fun. "See any bears?" he asked. "No," we answered. "But plenty of bear shit." As he drove out in his SUV with his dog seated upright by his side, he waved to us. What I've grudgingly grown to appreciate about living in the small community of the Catskills is that you encounter the people whom you demonize in public debates. You learn that they can be civil, perhaps even helpful. We live among people, not just polarized issues.

At the lean-to Paul peeled off an outer blue coat that he tied around his waist. The trick to winter hiking is not to overheat and drench yourself in perspiration. When you stop, no matter how much you're wearing, nothing chills you like your own sweat. We began ascending the trail that ramped steadily up the hillside above the stream that flowed from the saddle below Haynes Mountain. As we gained elevation, we saw the ridge that would lead us out to Hiram's Knob. The valley gradually narrowed to the top, a pocket marsh of black mud and white snow below a stone outcropping like a wall. It seemed a charmed spot, an idyllic wild garden. After a break at the trail intersection in the saddle, we continued up to Haynes in our boots. Though deeper the snow still didn't require snowshoes.

Like many Catskill peaks Haynes didn't offer the summit experience of views or an obvious pinnacle, but it did have a flat rock where we sat for lunch amid the trees. Despite its ordinary appearance, I had an interesting story to share about this summit. I'd hiked here with Michael Kudish, the forest historian. From him, I'd learned that the fir trees I associated with ridges and summits wasn't necessarily a high-elevation species. Rather, the balsam fir had arrived with the boreal forest after the Ice Age. For some four thousand years it had grown everywhere in the landscape. In time the northern hardwood forest dominated by sugar maples and beeches invaded to crowd out the firs, leaving them to the worst growing areas, the high elevations with harsh weather and poor soils. To piece together this story of the past twelve thousand years, Mike has studied the clues available to him today. On Haynes he could see the last scraggly fir trees dying out under a hardwood canopy of black cherry, yellow birch, beech and red maple trees. In 1970, as a result of his graduate-student research in the Catskills, he'd predicted that these firs would be gone by the end of the millennium. Yet in 2006 we found firs still standing on Haynes. Not just surviving, but producing saplings. Apparently, the forest transition took longer than he'd previously thought. (Later, Mike reasoned that snow, ice, and wind storms did enough damage to the hardwoods to give the firs a fighting chance.)

I wish I could say that Paul Levine was as fascinated by this discovery as I'd been, watching Michael Kudish recalculate forest history that spring afternoon. But Paul wasn't. He was cold.

Winter lunches eaten while seated on a snowy rock are pleasant for five minutes. After that, you chew quickly in order to start moving again. After Paul packed away his thermos coffee that we'd shared, I took a compass bearing to Hiram's Knob for our bushwhack, which proved to be easy and flat for the first two miles. Though we had to skirt some brambles and step over fallen logs we made good time. Along the way I kept glancing through the scrim of bare forest trees toward the long gentle shoulder of Belleayre Mountain to the north. Most people know Belleayre for its ski center, a dozen-plus runs raked down its northern face, but the mountain as a whole is much larger and wilder. Michael Kudish has even found original-growth forest on Belleayre that has never been logged.

My impatience did me no good. I saw plenty of Belleayre, but no cell tower. After two miles we reached the end of our flat ridgeline. Ahead of us was a deep drop into a notch followed by a steep climb up Hiram's Knob, which wasn't a knob at all, but a rugged hill far more imposing than its three hundred feet of contour lines had suggested on the map. Paul wasn't pleased. The end of a long hike is not the place to plant a new peak in his way, not when he's happily and determinedly descending toward the car. Had he not been a nice guy, he might have refused to climb Hiram's Knob in search of my prize, my cell tower view. But he's tolerant. And I'd become a man on a mission. Our happy-go-lucky bushwhack was over. The time had arrived to find that stone for my slingshot. David took charge.

Starting down the northern side of the ridge, I stepped into the first substantial snowpack of the day. Paul skirted the snow by staying up to my left, but I enjoyed myself thoroughly, taking big sliding boot steps down the virgin slope. For all I knew, this would be my last chance at winter. So I had blast descending in the deep snow. Then I happened into an opening in the tree canopy. There it stood, a towering needle pale gold with sunlight rising up from the Belleayre forest. It was so thin that it hardly looked like a cell tower. Yet it had to be what I wanted. The arrow pointing to the future location of nineteen houses. Why wasn't I outraged?

The Catskill High Peaks offer many vistas where it's possible to believe that civilization hasn't intruded into the mountains blanketed with forest from top to bottom. You might spot a ribbon of road in a valley, a few glinting rooftops, but little more amid the unbroken greenery. The view I now had of Belleayre wasn't like that. If anything, it was the view of an older Catskills, the nineteenth century mountains that had pastures high up the hillsides to tree lines. The cell tower wasn't a needle stabbing the heart of the wilderness. It was an innocuous spire above a farm valley of blond fields. Plus, it was awfully far away, three miles as the crow flies. Would nineteen houses discretely tucked among trees be noticeable? Honestly? My deadly slingshot stone was, in truth, a pathetic little pebble. No photographer would find a dramatic expose shot from this distance. Not unless he cheated like crazy with a telescopic lens. The kind that picks out pimples at a hundred yards.

We climbed Hiram's Knob anyway. It had a table-topped boulder that served as an unofficial summit marker on otherwise flat ground. It had—surprise, surprise—forest trees everywhere, blocking most of the view of Belleayre, never mind trying to spot the cell tower again. I wandered down into the woods in hopes of discovering another good clearing, but soon realized that I could waste an hour looking for something that wouldn't help anyway. I wasn't meant to be David slaying Goliath on a bushwhack. The truth was, it had taken a dedicated group of activists leading an angry army of citizens to stop this project so far, and it would take their hard work again in the future. I didn't feel cheated, though. My fantasy had given us an excuse to explore a new corner of the Catskills. Paul and I now claimed Hiram's Knob as one of our peaks. Satisfied, we headed down toward the cars. We debated whether or not "No Trespassing" signs applied to us if they were on the side of a tree we didn't see.

# Emergency!

Will Nixon

THE ICE PATCH between the roots and trail stones didn't even look that slippery, not with dirt and leaves mixed into the milky gray remnant of winter under the hemlocks. Nor was Michael's fall dramatic. His boots slid down the gentle slope. He landed as if to do a push-up with his face down beside a small tree up at the corner of the ice. For a moment I thought nothing of it. We'd all but reached our destination, the white castle-like towers of ice catching the spray from Kaaterskill Falls, one of the classic sights in the Catskills. The morning couldn't have been prettier. A brilliant blue sky. An early spring nip in the air. The forest to ourselves. Hiking up the half mile trail, we'd found the dirt frozen but clear of snow. The warming sun would soon thaw the ground. Winter was finished. But when Michael rolled over I saw a grimace like I'd never seen.

"Oh, fuck," he agonized in a whisper. He lay rigid on his back in his puffy black jacket. His gloved right hand gripped his left elbow. "I can't believe this," he said, eyes squeezed shut in pain. He let out a feral groan. "It's my shoulder. It's dislocated." His left forearm was shaking. The inch of skin exposed at his wrist was quivering. He looked like he was being electrocuted. I didn't know what to do. But, fuck, I had to do something.

We hadn't even planned to be here. We were going to do another hike, a bushwhack from a road end to look for the stone remnants of a Revolutionary War-era Tory hideout below Round-top Mountain. But the road end had been heavily posted. A dog had barked moments after we'd gotten out of the car. Michael had decided to put safety ahead of valor. He'd suggested Kaaterskill Falls, instead. An easy hike. One to write about for the tourists. The people in sneakers, I thought. And it had been fairly easy, though the steep stone steps at the start had winded me fast. Yet

I'd soon caught my breath. We'd reached the steep forested amphitheater holding the half frozen Kaaterskill Falls, a cathedral-sized altarpiece to the transcendent feelings of wilderness solitude. But suddenly Heaven had become Hell. Michael lay on the ice, his face gnarled in pain. We were alone. I didn't know what to do. Michael's face was the color of cold bony knuckles.

Did I even dare touch him? Rigid and quaking? In the best of times Michael looks frail. Tall and thin, he has a stoop and hikes with a walking stick, a traditional wooden cane. Yet he floats along on his feet as if the stoop high in his back is a balloon. He walks more than anyone I know. He never complains, never needs to stop to catch his breath. I'd grown completely comfortable with him in the woods. But now after an innocuous slip he lay groaning as if a dying animal called from the dry cave of his throat. I was scared. He was in terrible agony. What would the wrong twist or shove do? But I had to touch him. I had to get him off the ice.

Maybe he suffered shock. After a few minutes he seemed clearer. He told me the pain was in his left shoulder. Squatting beside him, careful to plant my boots on rocks so I wouldn't slip on the ice, I laid one hand on his thin leg in black jeans, the other on his right shoulder, and helped slide him down the sluiceway of ice until he was past the smooth trail boulder to his left. Then I helped him sit up against the rock. After a minute, I helped again, reaching down his back to grab his belt and shift his butt a final foot off the ice. Michael weighed nothing. I wished I could just carry him out of here. But wishes were useless now. Pain overwhelmed Michael. It owned him. He couldn't move. He sat with his knees pulled up near his chest. His left hand rested on his left knee. His right hand clamped his left hand in place. His feral groans rose out of deep ache. I noticed a scrape above his left eyebrow under his olive brown hat rim, a bruise that wasn't bleeding, thank God. His fall had been much harder than it looked.

I carry not one, but two first aid kits. But damned if I knew what to do with them. I ripped the duct tape off my homemade kit in a Tupperware box, and a Kotex pad spilled out. Somewhere I'd read that it would be handy for soaking up blood from an injury. A lot of good it did me now. Years ago I'd taken a wilderness first aid course, a weekend spent thinking, "I'm not learning anything by taking notes and playacting with bandages. I need practical experience." Now I was having my fucking experience. I found an ace bandage. Maybe I'd tie Michael's arm in a sling, the proper procedure for a dislocated shoulder. Whom was I kidding? Monkey around with his arm while he sat in agony? I stuffed the bandage in my pocket. I fed Michael two Tylenols and squatted in front of him to grip his right shin and gaze into his eyes. I didn't know what I was doing. I just knew I had to be there for him.

"Thirty years of hiking," he said. "I've never had an injury."

"You'll be all right," I promised.

"Give me five minutes," he said. He believed that if he could numb the pain, he'd be able to walk out. I wished it was true. I'd use my sweater to tie his arm in a sling. But Michael couldn't move. Every few moments a pain surge pulled him back into himself, groaning and closing his eyes. I kept talking to pull him out. I wanted to see him open his eyes. But time was passing. Perhaps twenty minutes since the fall. Did I dare leave him to run down the trail for help? Did I dare wait longer doing nothing but gaze into his eyes? We were alone. Nobody was out on the trail. Then Michael did move. He leaned slightly and swung out his right hand to grab at a root. Was he trying to pull himself up? It was one of the weakest gestures I've ever seen. "You can't stand up," I said, relieving him of the responsibility of trying. "I'll be back as soon as I can."

I charged down that trail. God, did I feel empowered to be taking action at last. The trail stones and roots reassured me that Michael never would have been able to walk out on his own. In what seemed like five minutes I came around a trail bend to the view down through the trees of the U-bend in the road where Route 23A, hugging the steep side of Kaaterskill Clove, crosses the stream bridge. A car drove down around the bend almost in slow motion. Another curved up. By the time I scrambled up the embankment the road was quiet. The sun was bright on the pavement. The bare trees deep in the gully below the bridge appeared ready to bud. The far side of Kaaterskill Clove made a dark mountain wall under the blue sky. A beautiful day. Proof of the cruel indifference of the wild. This quiet was the last thing I wanted.

Should I walk up to my car parked around the bend to drive for help? Or was that a panicky idea? A stupid way of leaving Michael even farther behind?

Fortunately, a truck rounded the upper bend, slowly descending, leading a train of four or five cars. Years ago, hitchhiking, I learned how easy it is for vehicles to pass by. There was no chance of that this time. I walked out into the road, waving my arms. The driver, visible in his big windshield, braked the truck to a jerky halt and rolled down his window. "It's an emergency," I announced. "I have my friend, an older man, up the trail with a dislocated shoulder."

I wish I could say the driver reacted. He looked stone faced, grumpy, a guy just doing his job, but getting flagged down in the middle of a mountain curve. In hindsight I realize I was wildly judgmental. What I wanted, I guess, was a savior. He wasn't a savior. He was a man doing exactly what he needed to. He fished out a cell phone from his seat and handed it to me, and then pulled the truck off to the roadside.

My problem was that I never use cell phones. They feel like miniature toys in my hands. Did I need to press a dial button? A talk button? I pushed 911 which appeared on the digital screen. But I heard nothing. So I stopped another car. This driver said that he doubted he'd get reception. I returned the cell phone to the truck. Studying the screen, the driver confirmed that he didn't have a signal. He told me that he'd call 911 as soon as he got down the hill. I thanked him. I felt grateful. But seconds later I waved down an SUV heading up the road. "It's an emergency," I told the driver, a younger man with short hair who told me, "I'm on it," in a commanding voice, exactly what I needed to hear. He'd call from the top of the clove.

Relieved, I charged back up the trail. Fifty feet until I was winded by the steep stone steps. "I'm out of shape," I thought. "Why am I so fucking unprepared?" But there was nothing I could do. I had to walk. It must have taken me fifteen minutes to get back up to the first view of the frozen waterfalls through the trees. Where was Michael? The one thing I had learned in first aid class was that people with hypothermia will do crazy things. They'll strip off their clothes as their last act before freezing to death. Could the pain have driven Michael to crawl off for some foolish reason? I'd left him alone for so long. At the next rise, thank God, I saw him up ahead still seated on the trail, small and huddled by his rock. He hadn't moved. Not even his two hands on his left knee. I felt relieved. I told him that 911 calls were going out from both the top and the bottom of the clove. He nodded in appreciation, stoical in his pain. I sat down beside him to share the wait. We had a conversation unlike any we'd had before.

I wouldn't call it a deathbed conversation for, despite my fears, I knew that he was stable and that help was coming. But it was a conversation infused with an awareness of the fragility of life and the passage of years that are gone forever. If he had his life to do over, Michael said, he'd be a forest ranger or a classicist. Instead, he'd been a literary man and a bookstore owner in the East Village in the 1960's. "I hated the Sixties," he told me. Yet he'd lived in the midst of them, a friend of such Sixties literary figures as Ed Sanders, Ishmael Reed, and Samuel Delaney. He'd known Abbie Hoffman. He'd received a joint in the mail from the Yippies, one of a thousand sent out to launch their political campaign. He'd been to a rooftop party with Andy Warhol's crowd where he'd met one of the most beautiful women in his life: Candy Darling. "She, or he, was absolutely gorgeous," he recalled, still awed by Beauty. Everything he said had great poignancy. I felt incredibly protective, almost a part of Michael, except for the pain, which though excruciating for him, I couldn't feel at all. I just knew we had to keep talking.

"I've only felt pain like this twice in my life," he said. "When I passed kidney stones. And when I was stabbed."

Stabbed? I asked for the story. At an evening party at an East Village bookstore, his brother-in-law had charged out to the street to chase some unruly teens. Michael had followed and wound up in the emergency room. Lying in the crowded hospital, he'd overheard a doctor, performing triage, tell someone to treat him later. "He's not going to make it," the doctor said. "But I knew I was going to make it," Michael told me. He'd spent nine days in intensive care back then. He'd make it now.

It seemed like we'd waited half an hour. "I just want to see a big needle," Michael said. I envisioned a man in a white lab coat arriving up the trail bearing a four-foot-high hypodermic needle like a cross. But that was fantasy. Reality was the sunlight through the hemlocks, the spring nip in the air, the rushing sound of the stream, this serene spot on a beautiful day, our absolute need to get Michael out of here.

The second time I scouted down the trail, I met a policeman almost upon us, a young man in a wool hat huffing as badly as I had down at the bottom. He must have pushed himself all the way up here. "Whoa!" he said, catching his breath. But he didn't waste any time. He had his notebook, his walkie-talkie. He asked Michael if he thought he could walk out.

"If they give me a pain killer," Michael said. "It's my shoulder. My legs are fine."

"Do you have a pain killer?" I asked the officer.

He grinned and patted his hand on his pistol visible under his unzipped jacket. I appreciated his humor. I hope that Michael did, too. "No," said the officer turning serious. "I'm afraid they won't do that." The rescuers, I realized, wouldn't administer those drugs. Until now Michael had resisted the idea of being carried out. He had his pride. Yet the decision was unavoidable. "I've got a stretcher waiting down at the bottom," the officer said. He held his walkie-talkie, connected to help. "I hate to be a nuisance," Michael said. "Don't worry. They enjoy doing this." The officer's smile made me think that they really did, no matter how arduous the task might seem to the rest of us.

Within minutes the forest ranger had arrived, a young woman in a green uniform, followed by half a dozen men, ranging in age from their twenties to their fifties, in hardhats and daypacks, sweat shirts and jeans. One dropped off a red daypack, a huge first aid kit. Four walkie-talkies started squawking at once. One man wore a climbing harness around his legs and waist, as if prepared to climb up beside the waterfall. I wondered if this response wasn't overkill. Hardhats? Climbing gear? For a dislocated shoulder? But what did I know? The idiot with a Kotex pad in his first aid kit.

A young man in a gray sweatshirt and oval-framed glasses pulled on purple latex gloves and knelt beside Michael's left side. He immediately did what I hadn't dared. He took off Michael's puffy jacket. He touched Michael's left shoulder. He tried swinging Michael's left hand toward his chest to prepare for a sling, then placed it back on the knee when the pain proved too much. He was the expert we'd needed for the past hour and a half. Standing behind him, I noticed silver studs in both ears below his dark crewcut, a younger generation's style. Hell, he was almost a kid. Yet he was doing for Michael what I'd failed to do, addressing the injury. Suddenly I choked up, my calm facade a dam ready to burst with tears. Why? Relief, of course. But gratitude, more gratitude than I'd ever felt in my life. These strangers, these trained volunteers had rushed up here to save Michael. Nor did my emotions fade. The whole time I was with the rescue crew I had a crybaby bomb inside me ready to explode if I started talking, so I remained observant and quiet.

Our waiting wasn't done. The stretcher had to be carried up. With his puffy jacket tucked in his lap, Michael got chilly so we wrapped a plastic yellow emergency blanket around him, a colorful sight: Michael in a rumpled yellow mound with his head and dark olive hat sticking out. He was enduring his pain, silent save for an occasional groan. Our close connection was replaced by the jocular energy of the rescue squad. They weren't the kind of people I know in Woodstock. They were younger, short haired, feisty and loud, guys with equipment, guys with real jobs, unlike Michael and me who've spent our lives wrapped up in books. One wore camouflage shorts past his knees to his calf tattoos. Michael asked, "Aren't you cold?" "Nah," someone else answered. "He wears shorts all the time."

Eventually, the stretcher arrived, carried on the back of a man overheated in a yellow fireman's suit. I wondered again, why so much equipment? Why wear a yellow sweat suit? But what did I know? The poet befuddled by a cell phone. These men were prepared. They arrived ready for anything.

Quickly, the group assembled the stretcher that came in two halves, an oval metal frame with black webbing, plus a hard plastic blue board, also in two halves, that lay in the stretcher. Michael's moment of truth had come. After sitting motionless for so long in his least painful position, he was lifted onto the blue board, then had to lie down on his back. His groans grew anguished and loud, almost a wail. Jarring his shoulder had to be torturing him. They lay his left arm at his side padded by his puffy jacket. My daypack became his pillow. They strapped him in with what looked like six or eight seat belts. The man in a climbing harness, I now learned, hadn't worn it as a fashion statement. His black daypack contained a blue climbing rope that he tied onto the stretcher by Michael's head and ran through a belay system at his waist. He added an important backstop for safety. Several times on the way down he belayed the stretcher down steep rocks or steps while the carriers found their footing.

I carried Michael's hat and walking stick, two indelible parts of his identity. I even tried on the hat for a moment, but decided that was going too far. His head lay bare on the stretcher with tussled up wisps of gray hair. His head looked larger than I'd realized, but I wondered if I'd ever seen him without a hat. Maybe not. The accident had drawn me into his life in new ways.

The stretcher carriers stopped every few hundred yards to switch sides or change to fresh carriers. By now fifteen or sixteen rescuers had arrived to take turns. Halfway down we'd met a young group from Palenville in yellow firemen's suits. Their bulky uniforms hadn't slowed them down in the least. They were eager to join the rescue.

When we came to the trail corner with the view of the U-shaped bend in the road, I saw half a dozen vehicles parked at the roadside, including a big box-shaped red ambulance and a big box-shaped white ambulance. I was amazed. An army had turned out for Michael. I verged on babbling tears. I knew I was witnessing something rare. I'd never been among so many people, complete strangers, doing so much to help someone in desperate need. Near the hillside bottom yet more rescuers had set up an orange rope system around a thick tree trunk to help belay the stretcher down the stone steps. There must have been two dozen people involved in this rescue between the carriers and the crew waiting at the bottom.

Before lowering Michael down a staircase built into the hillside, the men laid his stretcher on the ground. One held out his forearm to shade Michael's eyes. Michael said something I couldn't hear. Four or five guys burst into laughter. "He's telling jokes!" one announced. Through his pain Michael had been able to join their jocular camaraderie.

After the steady but slow descent, things happened rapidly as soon as Michael's stretcher was laid on the pavement. A woman paramedic, who'd wheeled over a stretcher bed with white sheets, reached under his gray sweater to feel his shoulder. I couldn't help but stare at the exposed skin by his neck but felt relieved not to see the injury itself. She wrapped his arm in a sling. The men lifted Michael onto the table bed where he sat up with a back support. "Will," he called over to me. "Bring my jacket. It's got my wallet." A minute later the white ambulance pulled into the road and briefly slowed as the driver lowered his window. "Kingston Hospital!" he barked at me. And was gone.

Traffic had backed up at both ends of the U-shaped bend. All this commotion for Michael's shoulder. All this effort to save him. All this caring. As the forest ranger drove me up to my parked car, I didn't start bawling, but did ask her for everyone's name so that we could thank them personally. I'd sensed from her and others that they saw themselves as simply doing their jobs. But I knew that my job in the days ahead would be to express my gratitude. I'd never seen such altruistic willingness to put everything aside to answer an emergency call. These men and women had saved Michael's life.

Then I fucked up a final time. On the Thruway from Saugerties to Kingston, as I sped along with Michael's jacket in my passenger seat, I grew impatient at the length of the drive. Kingston couldn't be this far, could it? Minutes later I recognized a green road sign on an overhead bridge. Kingston? Hell! I was on my way to New Paltz. Somehow with my mind aswirl I'd driven right past the Kingston exit. Even in hindsight I can't remember having seen it. So much for me in an emergency.

I reached the Kingston Hospital half an hour late. It didn't seem to matter. I found Michael in the corner bay of the emergency room on a bed with a tube in his arm and a wall monitor tracking his heart beat. He was still in pain and still dressed in his hiking boots, jeans, gray sweater, and a red scarf I hadn't noticed before. His left arm remained in its sling. Leaf bits were snagged in his sweater. He was still groaning despite having received morphine in the ambulance. I untied the sling bandage pinching his neck but could do nothing more. The nurse injected a fresh needle of painkiller into Michael's arm tube, but it wasn't enough. He tried to keep talking, but drifted off.

Sadly, his ordeal was far from over. Sondra, his wife, reached the hospital at four in the afternoon and called me after 11:30 that night to report that Michael had suffered for hours while several doctors tried and failed to pop his shoulder back in place. Though given painkillers, Michael had never gotten the big needle that he'd longed for back up on the trail. Finally, another doctor put him under general anesthesia and slipped his shoulder into its socket. Now, days later, he tells me that he's having trouble sleeping while sitting up in his arm sling. But he has our next hike planned. Magic Meadow on the flank of Overlook Mountain. First, though, we'll wait for the stream between the road and the meadow to go down. We'll want to be able to cross it without any trouble.

||||||||||||||||||||||||||||||||||||||||||||||||||||||||||||||||||||||||||||||||||||||

If you visit Kaaterskill Falls, as you should, you'll be amazed that such a frightening accident could happen in such a popular place that draws visitors who may be casual hikers at best. For almost two hundred years, the falls have been one of the most famous sites in the Catskills. The bottom is reached by a half-mile trail. On Route 23A between Palenville and Haines Falls there's a parking area a quarter of a mile uphill from this trailhead. –W.N.

||||||||||||||||||||||||||||||||||||||||||||||||||||||||||||||||||||||||||||||||||||||

# Carried Out

Michael Perkins

YOU NEVER THINK it can happen to you.

In thirty years of long solo hikes, from the Catskill Peaks to the Cornwall Cliffs, I had never fallen, never returned home with wounds more serious than scratches and insect bites.

But I had fallen hard, and now here I was being carried out of Kaaterskill Clove on a stretcher and groaning rhythmically because it seemed to ease the blast furnace of pain roaring in my dislocated, broken left shoulder.

How had it happened? I was wearing cleats on my boots and stepping carefully—but I was also talking with Will, and looking forward to seeing the magnificent, frozen falls again. The ice was waiting.

Then I noticed that my cleats were jammed into a rescue worker's chest, and he didn't seem to mind. I realized that I must have put them on inside out—spikes into soles rather than ice.

*Stupid. Careless.* I berated myself and groaned loudly for the hundredth time. We like to blame ourselves—if we can't blame others—because we like to think that the world makes sense— that "there are no accidents." But there are.

The rescue workers put me down so they could rest. These were men who had volunteered to risk their safety for a stranger. I stared up at the pale blue sky and the stippled outlines of tree tops. Suddenly I was overwhelmed with gratitude. The sun in my face, the the sound of the stream rushing below, the men talking, the look of concern on Will's face. I thought of Natasha Richardson's freakish, fatal skiing accident the week before. I was lucky. I was alive. I would heal.

# Postscript

Will Nixon

SEVERAL WEEKS AFTER THE ACCIDENT I met Stephen Tuomey for coffee in Saugerties. "You were the guy carrying the belay rope, right?" I asked. No longer in his blue helmet, no longer handling the rope coming out of his daypack, no longer preoccupied by his command duties during the rescue, he was recognizable but different, relaxed and friendly with a big boyish smile. I wondered if, as a kid, he'd been the one in the neighborhood with a cherubic face and a devilish side, the boy who organized all the fun. Now he had a life full of adult responsibilities. He worked as a Saugerties police dispatcher. For twenty-seven years, he'd volunteered for the Tannersville Rescue Squad, becoming the Assistant Chief who oversaw thirty active members from Haines Falls, Hunter, and Tannersville. More than two dozen people had helped with Michael's rescue. I wanted to thank Stephen again for what they'd done. Plus I had questions.

I learned that Michael had been in shock, more than I realized. "He was white as a ghost," Stephen said. "He was shivering." That concerned the rescuers as much as did the dislocated shoulder. Adam Goodrich had been the young man administering care, feeling the injured shoulder, then taking Michael's pulse to see if the dislocation blocked blood flow, which, thankfully, it hadn't. A certified first responder, Adam had spent many hours in first aid training. These volunteers gave a lot more of their time than taken up by the actual rescues.

I'd regretted not having a strong pain killer in my first aid kit. To my surprise, Stephen said that I'd done the right thing by only giving him Tylenol. As terrible as the pain had been for Michael, the rescuers relied on his moaning as a medical monitoring system. If his injury had gotten worse while doped up, he wouldn't have felt it, and they wouldn't have known. The proper person to administer serious drugs was the EMT.

Why so much equipment? The gear bags? The yellow suits? The helmets? It turned out that my urgent but no doubt panicky call for help into several vehicle windows had gotten garbled by the time the rescuers arrived on the scene. They didn't know what to expect. They'd come ready to rescue someone from a cliff, if necessary. The suits protected their clothes against blood and dirt. The hardhats were in case they'd called in a helicopter, which could hover below the falls to lower a cable to hoist a stretcher. Once a tool bag had fallen out of the helicopter. So the helmets were precautionary.

Talking with Stephen I appreciated how much these volunteers did. They trained. They performed rescues. On beautiful weekends when the rest of us headed outdoors for fun they waited by their beepers for trouble. The emotional roller coaster that I'd gone through with Michael's rescue made me realize the psychological stress that these men must face when handling gruesome injuries, even death. Their cure for this stress, said Stephen, was "dark humor, as dark as can be." They didn't want to take traumatic feelings home to their families.

They made another sacrifice that surprised me: Kaaterskill Falls. They found little joy in a place that for everyone else is one of the Catskill's grandest attractions. To them, the amphitheater was an accident waiting to happen. Fifteen to twenty times a year, they marched up the trail to rescue someone, ranging from ice climbers to neophytes in flip-flops who'd scrambled up the steep hillside above the trail only to fall and roll down the rocky slope. Only once has Stephen walked out to the top of the falls for fun with his family. They took a trail that reaches the falls from above. Sure enough, by the end of the afternoon he was hiking back in from below with a rescue team on an emergency call.

My final question: what was the joke Michael told while lying in the stretcher near the bottom? I'd heard the laughter but not the joke itself. "That came out of the blue," said Stephen with a grin. "One long moan all the way down. Then he said that." The squad was still laughing about it. I won't repeat the joke, though it starts with a man wearing a frog on his head and ends with a funny punch line. "He told us that as a form of thanks," Stephen said. Michael was ahead of me. The best I could do was pay for the coffee.

# WANDERING THOUGHTS
# AND SUNBAKED OPINIONS

# In Praise of Walking Sticks

Michael Perkins

I CAN'T IMAGINE going for a walk without a stick in hand. It must stand about thirty-eight inches, be light but strong, and fit in my hand as if it emerged from the womb with me. It helps me to balance, it is a useful tool against pests, it helps push impediments from my path, and above all, it keeps me company. Henry Miller called his bicycle his best friend, and I consider my collection of walking sticks close company.

Yet I've found that most hikers in our area don't use them. I suspect that people who go stickless do so because they fear that they will be considered infirm; almost everyone calls a walking stick a cane, and canes are geezer aids.

The ancestry of the stick goes back to the caves. A staff is hierophantic—Moses parted the sea with one. A stick has always been a defensive weapon, but in the eighteenth and nineteenth centuries it became an article of dress for gentlemen. Fashionable men carried elegant sticks topped with ivory and silver—sticks that often concealed swords or jiggers of brandy.

The philosopher Alan Watts brought a dress stick with him on his first trip to America. When a customs official inquired if he was infirm, Watts replied, "No, my good man, this is for swank."

In any collection of sticks there are some for work and some for swank. Each one is a souvenir of a walking trip. I found my first walking stick at a county fair in Yorkshire in 1969. I had just visited the Haworth home of the Bronte sisters, so I named it Heathcliff. Then there is the blackthorn stick I bought in Bristol to commemorate a walk on Offa's Dike in Wales, and the carved stick I bought to celebrate a hot walk across half the island of Tobago. For swank, there is the Chinese lacquer stick I bought in Florence two decades ago.

Anyone can pick up a stick in the woods, carve it, and have an ideal trail partner. A stick requires no upkeep, never complains, will go anywhere, and doesn't mind when you balance it in the palm of your hand or on the tip of your nose. What more can you ask from a friend?

# In Praise of the Catskill 3500 Club

Will Nixon

UPON MOVING into a Catskills log cabin in the summer of 1996, one of the best things I did was to join up with the Catskill 3500 Club. Before then, while living in Hoboken or Manhattan, I'd been an avid day hiker, catching the bus to Tuxedo Park to explore Harriman State Park or the train to Cold Spring to climb Breakneck Ridge. Typically, I went with friends, but a few times I tried Sierra Club hikes. Big mistake. Let's face it: I'd been an Eagle Scout, a winter camper, a backpacker in the High Sierras during my college years in California. What was I now doing among amateurs in blue jeans, people who didn't know that "cotton kills," or at least that wet jeans are miserably cold in the rain compared to light wool or synthetics? Then there was the proverbial guy with Coke-bottle-thick eyeglasses. Not just the glasses. One of the lenses kept popping out and vanishing into the ground cover leaves. For minutes at a time, he groped on his hands and knees, then quit with a whiny vow to soldier on with one lens. With that lens and the gap for his bare eye his black frames were a geek variation on the pirate's eye patch. The leader scolded him to keep searching. I stood by, silent and seething. I'd grown up in a dysfunctional family. I hadn't come on this hike to forge a new one among strangers.

Who knows? Maybe I was too young for hiking groups. By the time I reached the Catskills, I was almost forty, newly separated from a sixteen year relationship and marriage, determined to make a new life for myself in the mountains, and lonely. Somehow I found the Catskill 3500 Club—in those pre-Google days, how did I find anything? I don't remember—and on a Saturday morning at the end of August I met a dozen people gathered at a pullout on Route 42 north of Shandaken for a bushwhack up Halcott Mountain. Until then, I'd never heard of Halcott. But isn't that the point of the Catskill 3500 Club?

Founded in 1962, the Club recognizes people who have climbed all thirty-five peaks above 3500 feet, plus four of them again in winter to prove they're not fair-weather hikers. You may accomplish this feat however you like: solo, barefoot, with dog, without, in one month, over fifty years, by the age of eight, or by the age of seventy-three. At the end you receive an oval green patch, a certificate, and a membership number. But what I liked best about the Club was that every Saturday and Sunday, except during hunting season, it led hikes up one of the thirty-five peaks.

Our guide for Halcott was a chemistry professor from Oneonta who wore a white headband and knew his way with a map and compass. Because the summit was little more than a mile from the road we would make a full day it by first climbing Northeast Halcott along the same ridgeline. Though I wasn't a virgin at bushwhacking, I was awfully new to it. Other than a prominent roadside boulder offering a miniature waterfall, these woods appeared featureless without a trail. I wouldn't have known where to go. But this crew didn't hesitate. The hard chargers started up the hillside, the leaders in friendly competition to find the route with the fewest stinging nettles.

To many people, the word "bushwhacking" conjures up images of British explorers in pith helmets slashing through jungle vines with machetes. In the Catskills it simply means trailless hiking. At times, as I'd learn in the coming months, it can be torturous, especially in the stunted spruce and fir forests at high elevations. Densely jammed together, these trees are thick with stiff dead branches that snap at you like nasty little whips. The first time one thwapped me full force on a nipple I flashed on a shop awning in Greenwich Village that advertised piercings "with pain or without." Never in this lifetime, I decided, was I getting a nipple ring. Minutes later, another branch stung my other nipple to give me a matching pair. To maintain my sanity while shoving through these woody thickets with my head ducked low and my arms raised to protect my eyes, I recited Zippy the Pinhead's mantra: "Are we having fun yet?" Oddly enough, the answer was often, "Hell, yes! " Especially when we stumbled out of the conifers to find the orange canister nailed to the summit tree.

Out in the open forests, however, bushwhacking can be a pleasure. You learn to appreciate the value of the "Forever Wild" Catskill Forest Preserve that has allowed forests to grow back to towering maturity over many decades, even a century in places. Under these green cathedral canopies the understory can be surprisingly easy to traverse, though you must find your footing on the rocky ground. Paying attention to every step, however, immersed me in the forest more than did trail hiking that let my mind wander. Only on bushwhacks, for instance, did I notice those big woody tree fungus that could have made shields for trolls. On footpaths I was too busy daydreaming.

So the Catskills 3500 Club introduced me to bushwhacking, which I hadn't done in Harriman State Park or anywhere else. On Halcott and subsequent trips I took out my map and compass to learn from the leaders until I felt confident enough to try navigating for myself. Some seventeen of the thirty-five peaks are trailless, so I spent lots of time in the woods as they naturally are, a green complexity with challenges and surprises, not a forest bisected and tamed by trails. Bushwhacking made me feel enterprising and adventurous, no longer a mule following a dirt track.

I also liked the people on the Halcott hike. There was a lanky young distance runner who used hiking poles and hopped along on light feet that belied his hiking books. After hearing that he'd bushwhacked twenty-plus miles in a day, I considered him the John Muir of the Catskills. A fellow from Albany with a red bandanna loosely knotted around his neck was an Adirondack Forty-Sixer for having climbed the forty-six peaks above 4,000 feet. Now he was completing the Catskills. (A phenomenon that I encountered on Club hikes was Adirondack Envy. Sooner or later somebody told a story that make the Adirondacks seem bigger and better than the Catskills. Which I later learned as a journalist in the Adirondacks was both true and not true.) These folks were the peak baggers, the rock hoppers, the true athletes of the wild.

Yet I also met casual hikers, such as a friendly blonde nurse who taught me a few flowers like the blue bead clintonia, a common plant at higher elevations that has lance-shaped leaves and a straight stalk with three or four blueberry-like fruits. She warned me, however, that these berries were poisonous. Instead, we tasted lemony wood sorrel that grew like clover mats in the forest shade. Earlier in the day, she'd pocketed  raspberry leaves to brew into tea to help alleviate menstrual cramps. I enjoyed learning such things. For sixteen years I'd been an urban elitist who believed that the City was the center of action, the capitol of ambition and success. By leaving, I feared I might be giving up on myself. Now I was meeting upstaters who led perfectly satisfying lives without knowing the subway lines. Instead, they knew about flowers and bushwhacking, knowledge I hungered to acquire. Meeting new people on a hike felt more satisfying than standing in a stranger's living room, chatting over white wine at a party. That evening at my cabin I filled out the first line in my Club tally sheet with the comment "fantastic." The next day I climbed Peekamoose on a Club hike. The leader showed me the charred seam in a tree trunk left by a lightning strike. Everyone had something to share. The Club was my Welcome Wagon.

After that weekend I was off and running. Sure, I met gear heads, peak baggers, people obsessed with hiking accomplishments as if they led no other lives. But I also met teachers, lawyers, world travelers, computer programmers, a volunteer fireman, a gas station owner, an Air Force technician, New Jersey commuters, Albany bureaucrats, Long Islanders who'd left home at five in the morning to reach the trailhead on time. My only surprise was meeting so few fellow Catskillians. To live in these mountains but not climb them was like living in Manhattan but not eating Thai or Brazilian. Maybe my neighbors feared the mountains as places best left to the bears and the mysteries. So I met folks from New Paltz and Queens,

Poughkeepsie and Colonie. On one hike I made two friends—one from Tribeca in Manhattan, the other from Ridgefield, Connecticut—who became my hiking partners for years to come.

That list of thirty-five summits also sent me out to places I wouldn't have gone if not for the peaks. There was the beautiful Spruceton Valley leading out to West Kill, Hunter, and Rusk that made me think of the West because of its grass valley that sloped up to the forest line. (Once, bushwhacking down from a non-Thirty-Fiver beyond Rusk, my friend and I crossed a bright new compound of log buildings with its own helipad. "Montana has reached the Catskills!" we declared.) Then there was Maplecrest, the white clapboard ghost town on the way to the Blackheads, a hamlet later restored as an arts center by the Catskill Mountain Foundation. And the epic hour-long drive across the wildest Catskills on Route 47 to reach the trailhead in Denning, a distance less than ten miles from my cabin as the crow flies. That area has been called the Alaska of Ulster County. Perhaps I would have discovered these places on Sunday drives. Except that I never took Sunday drives.

By the end I had peak bagging fever. To finish before the Club's annual dinner in April, I climbed eight peaks in March, some of them solo. My final pair were Bearpen and Vly, two more unknowns if not for the list. On a gray Sunday morning after parking past a farm I hiked up a gravel road rutted by water runoff to the saddle between the two peaks. A tarpaper-covered hunting cabin stood off to the side. Though I had snowshoes strapped to my day pack, I didn't need them, since the snow had melted except under the shrubs. I followed my compass bearing to the top of Bearpen, which had an open forest spread flat across an acre or two cloaked in fog. I walked around until satisfied that I'd crossed the summit, wherever it might be. Back down in the saddle my bearing up Vly marched me straight up the hill to a summit clearing of winter plant stalks bordered by gnarly trees. An easy Thirty-Fiver, but immensely satisfying. In six months I'd climbed them all. I hadn't been so dedicated to a goal in years. At the Club banquet several weeks later, I received my handshake and certificate at the podium with a surge of pride I hadn't felt since college graduation. Completing those peaks had transformed me from an urban neophyte trying cabin life—when I'd asked a local where to buy kindling for my wood stove, he 'd told me to look under the trees—into a Catskillian who'd seen the mountains from all sides. (Adirondack Envy? After finishing the Forty-Sixers years later, I skipped the dinner. As much as I'd loved the Adirondacks, I hadn't changed my life by hiking them.)

In time I went on to climb the peaks a second and third time, or a sixth and seventh, as I helped friends complete their thirty-five or simply returned to favorites. Yet I must confess that I haven't taken a Club hike in years. Nor do I feel the call of the High Peaks. Instead, I've explored the Low Peaks of Woodstock with a handful of friends, none of whom belongs to the Catskill 3500 Club. They may be too polite to say so themselves, but let me summarize their objections. Who wants to be herded like a pack animal? Why hike with strangers when you've got friends? What's with checking off peaks from a list like groceries at the supermarket? Shouldn't we hike to leave behind our competitive, goal-obsessed egos that distract us from the natural wonders to be found it we stop, look, and listen to the forest?

I smile in hearty agreement. Then I ask, not so subtly, if they've climbed North Dome and Sherrill, Graham and Double-top, Rocky and Lone. It becomes clear that they haven't seen half the Catskills I've seen. The Catskill 3500 Club got me out there. They made these mountains my home.

The website is Catskill-3500-Club.org. To join the hikes, you'll need to subscribe to the Club's newsletter. Details at the website. The Rip Van Winkle Hikers go out on weekdays as well as weekends. They're at newyorkheritage. com/rvw/. The Catskill Mountain Club at catskillmountainclub.org sends out announcements for hikes and other outdoor events.–W.N.

# Peak Bragging

Michael Perkins

PEAK BAGGING—the activity pursued by the Catskill 3500 Club—is, to my mind, peak bragging. It is antithetical to my notion of why we enter the wilderness, which is to encounter the transcendent—to be reminded of our insignificance, to strive, not for a badge in competition with others, but with ourselves.

A mountain should be approached reverently. It is church enough for the climber who has a sense of awe. I never arrive at a summit without feeling I have entered heaven's precincts.

Peak bagging follows from the noxious flatlander belief in the conquest of nature and the laws of competition—from the wish to put humanity's stamp on all creation.

I don't know how many of the Catskill High Peaks I have climbed—not all of them by a long shot. I hope to climb more in the company of a friend like Will, but I won't keep a record, or join an organization.

We'll reach the peaks without fanfare.

# Not the *Underground Woodstock Walk Book*

Will Nixon

FOR THE PAST DOZEN YEARS, my friend Paul Levine has driven over from Connecticut once a month to further our explorations of the Catskills. By now he has climbed the one hundred and two highest peaks in the region. (Why not an even one hundred? Don't ask. Paul has done not only East Gray but the false East Gray, two hills most hikers have never heard of.) We repeatedly face the challenge of finding a mountainside that he hasn't ascended in fifty years of roaming the Catskills, yet we always come up with something. The only hike that has foiled us—twice now—has been climbing Platte Clove past a series of a dozen waterfalls. It can be done. I've read e-mailed descriptions and seen a hand-drawn map. But each time that we've started at the bottom in West Saugerties, following paths used by swimmers to reach the lower falls, we've proceeded for several hours along the embankments or out on the rocky streambed itself only to meet our match high up a steep hillside that must be climbed to avoid a waterfall but scares us half to death. With dirty hands from grabbing roots, muddy pants knees, and conifer needles collared inside our shirts, we've retreated down the slope, vowing to return with better directions.

Which isn't to say these hikes weren't successful. Platte Clove is one of the wildest places in the Catskills, a gorge that has the feeling of ruins once lost and now partially rediscovered with unofficial trails to secluded waterfalls. The one that stopped Paul and me stood seventy-feet tall. Standing under it for water to pummel my shoulders was like taking a shower meant for Paul Bunyan. Wild places made you feel bigger, more daring, surprised at what you can do. And the trails only reached the lower falls. Paul and I continued past them, feeling like pioneers, easily advancing along the cobblestone streambed, then jungle gyming around giant boulders tumbled together in steep sections. Who knew how many people came through here in a year? The only intrusions were the occasional car tires that idiots had rolled off Plate Clove Road far up the hillside. (I'll confess to having once been such an idiot. Walking Platte Clove Road, one of the great road hikes in our area, I hopped over the guardrails to explore the garbage dumps half camouflaged down in the woods. It was amazing what I found: a Ping-Pong table, an old neon bar sign, a black sedan balanced upside down on its roof on a boulder. Amid so much trash, I gave in to the temptation to stand a tire upright and push off it down the hill. The last I saw of it, the tire was happily gaining speed and bounding off rocks, a daredevil no tree would stop.)

The first time we descended, Paul and I unwittingly veered off on a side trail near the bottom and came up to a ranch house lawn on Platte Clove Road. Another hundred feet and we'd be on the road, walking the rest of the way down to our cars. We didn't make it. A young man rushed out to stop us at the edge of his yard. Bare chested and skinny, but with a weightlifter's tight biceps and pecs, he wore blue jeans and carried a beer bottle, a casual touch, but he also wore a hunting rifle strapped to his back. For the first and last time (so far), Paul and I were confronted for trespassing. Not that Paul was intimidated. Over the course of his business career, he's faced everything from tropical jungles to angry public hearings in Brooklyn. Friendly as ever, he all but invited the guy to join us on our next hike. I explained that we'd arrived at his yard by mistake. To no avail. The young man wasn't unpleasant, but his rifle made his point: no way we were crossing his property. So we backtracked and found the path down to our cars. In fact, I felt sorry for the guy. Why was he home at 2:30 on a weekday afternoon lifting weights, drinking beer, and armed guarding his property against middle-aged day hikers? Was he out of work? Mad at the world? Whatever. By the time Paul and I reached our cars we'd transformed the encounter into a fresh tale for our growing repertoire of hiking lore.

Only once in our dozen years has Paul invited me to hike in Connecticut. Not that I haven't been to his house many times for parties. But when we put on our boots we want to be in the Catskills. Yet one mild December day I drove over to his house in Ridgefield for a morning ramble through the wooded valleys and ridges to be followed by a holiday lunch with his wife, a warmhearted woman who knows better than to take our hiking braggadocio too seriously. What impressed me that day wasn't the hike itself, though we followed a pretty route past a pond and over several ridges, but the *Ridgefield Walk Book*. The Catskills has hiking guides that describe the region's trails in the High Peaks. But a town volume? What would a *Woodstock Walk Book* look like?

Not much, I'm afraid. Of the forty-three thousand and two hundred acres in Woodstock, some fourteen thousand are owned and protected by the state's Catskill Forest Preserve, New York City for watershed lands, the City of Kingston as reservoir properties around Cooper Lake, the Town of Woodstock, or the Woodstock Land Conservancy and the Open Space Institute, two private groups. That's one third of our town. Yet on this land you can find a grand total of six public trails. There are loops of a mile or two at Sloan Gorge, the Comeau Property, and Wilson State Park. There's the busy trail up Overlook and the quiet trail up the back of Mount Tremper. Finally, the Mount Guardian trail is available to the public but doesn't appear on hiking maps. To be generous, let's add the trailhead at the end of Mink Hollow Road, though the trail quickly leaves Woodstock for Greene County.

Ridgefield, in contrast, has about thirty-five hundred protected acres divided among more than seventy separate parcels. More than twenty-five properties have trails described in the *Ridgefield Walk Book*. Granted, many paths take half an hour to complete, none over two and a half hours. Nobody will find a weekend backpack in the *Ridgefield Walk Book*. But the residents do have two dozen places spread about town to stretch their legs in the evening, go birding early on a spring morning, or take the kids out to hunt for salamanders and frogs. Many Woodstockers looking for comparable experiences have the Comeau, the Comeau, and the Comeau.

Pathetic, isn't it? That a town with so much public land should offer so few public trails. Call it the Outdoors Abstinence Policy. Enjoy the gorgeous scenery. But stay on the roads. Yet if anyone still harboring that old Sixties spirit were to compile an *Underground Woodstock Walk Book*, they'd put Ridgefield's efforts to shame. Our forests are crisscrossed with old woods roads and unmarked paths that constitute a *de facto* trail system far more extensive than any found on maps. Once you find your way into this system you can walk for hours. But these routes cross private property to reach public lands, or may remain entirely on private parcels. Somebody with a rifle slung across his shoulders has every right to stop you from trespassing.

What's to be done about this conundrum? The public reformer in me cries out for a petition, a committee, a campaign for Woodstock to expand its public trail system with the cooperation of private landowners. The utopian in me has a bolder idea: let Woodstock secede from the United States to rejoin the British empire. Not only would we get national health care. We'd invoke the public right to walk across private lands, so long as we closed pasture gates behind us. Woodstock wouldn't even need many pasture gates.

Then the hiker in me says, "Give it a rest, buddy. Let's go for a walk." And I do, content to appreciate Woodstock for what it is, a mixture of heavily used trails on Overlook and at the Comeau, and unmapped woods routes that I seem to have for myself. Why spoil the solitude by advertising these paths in public guides? Why ruin the fun I've had exploring them on my own? Not every walk should be mapped in advance. The *Ridgefield Walk Book* is nice. It has pretty illustrations of marsh marigolds and sensitive ferns. But I prefer the Wild Wild West that's Woodstock.

One winter day I led Paul Levine over Mount Tobias. I had a theory that a dead-end lane off Wittenberg Road would lead us up to a woods road that I knew of on the ridgeline. From the ridge we'd cross the summit and drop down to Cooper Lake. My theory, alas, didn't last past the final house after which we found ourselves wandering in the woods without a trail in sight. Which, for us, wasn't unusual, though we'd be loathe to admit it. We're fools for theories and rumors about woods roads that we never find. So I pulled out my compass and set a bearing for the ridgetop, which wasn't hard to find since it lay straight uphill. The biggest challenge was keeping Paul from straying off on what he hoped might be trails. He hates the mindless certitude of a compass bearing.

After lunch and coffee on a cold summit rock we started down toward Cooper Lake two miles distant. Even from the summit hump we caught glimpses of the silvery lake through the bare winter forest. Still, it took more than an hour to navigate down the hillside, which in typical Catskills fashion had gently sloped benches interrupted by small broken-up cliffs that demanded downward scrambling. We passed under giant hemlocks, successfully avoided the sprawling mountain laurel thickets, and walked into a meadow slope that I recognized from previous explorations. (Somewhere in here I unwittingly stepped through the worst prickly plant of my life. Those peppercorn-size seeds sharper than Velcro later took me several hours and a pair of pliers to pull out of my pants and fleece jacket.) Cooper Lake lay in clear view in the near distance beyond the valley forest, a metallic serving tray under the gray sky.

By the bottom of the meadow we'd lost sight of the lake behind the trees. In ten minutes we'd be there. I let my compass hang from my string necklace and followed a stream down to the bottom. We'd all but finished. Yet somehow in those ten minutes we managed to miss Cooper Lake by a quarter of a mile. We emerged in a swamp along the stream that flows west from the lake. How could that be? We'd seen the lake straight ahead. We'd followed a stream. What could possibly go wrong?

Don't think I wasn't delighted. It was as if we'd walked through a space warp to arrive in an unexpected location beyond our control. (Either that, or we'd goofed up.) It was an experience to add to our compendium of hiking lore: the mysterious dimension lurking in the Cooper Lake woods. Who knows? Maybe somebody else walking through that spot had found themselves in Phoenicia. Or New Jersey. That wasn't a discovery we would have made had we known where we going thanks to a *Walk Book*. Sometimes ignorance is the best guide.

|||||||||||||||||||||||||||||||||||||||||||||||||||||||||||||||||||||||||||||||||||||||||||||||||||||||

At the top of Platte Clove you may walk down to an impressive waterfall without risking life or limb. The Platte Clove Preserve owned by the Catskill Center for Conservation and Development is a pretty property with a red cottage and a trail down to waterfalls. The Catskill Center asks that you park a bit east of the Preserve at the trailhead parking area that's up a dirt road on the north side of Platte Clove Road. The walk back to the Preserve takes a few minutes. –W.N.

|||||||||||||||||||||||||||||||||||||||||||||||||||||||||||||||||||||||||||||||||||||||||||||||||||||||

# A Walk into the Past

Michael Perkins

IN THE SUMMER OF 1988 I took a walk of about ten miles from my
house in Glenford to the Ashokan Field Campus. It was, quite literally,
a walk into the past, because my destination was the the year 1840.

No telephones. No plastic. No internal combustion engines.
No radio or television. No modern distractions. Seven days of
quiet. Erase almost two centuries of technology, and step into the
world of the buckskinners' rendezvous.

Over two hundred people took a giant step together back
into American frontier history when the the Great Northeast
Territories Rendezvous, sponsored by the Marbletown Sportsmen's Clubs and the New York State Muzzleloaders Association,
was held at the Ashokan Field Campus in Shokan. They came
from Pennsylvania and Rhode Island, from Olean and Queens
to participate in the third annual week-long re-creation of the
daily life of a legendary period, when Daniel Boone, Kit Carson,
Jeremiah Johnson and Davy Crockett walked out into the freedom of the wilderness to live like Indians, like the Cherokee
or the Sioux, and depended for their lives on their single shot
black powder long rifles.

At Old Sturbridge Village and Colonial Williamsburg, history is presented in pageant form. It can be visited. It is tourist-
friendly. At a rendezvous, history is relived from the inside out.
Buckskinners—that is what these new mountain men and women
call themselves—build a time machine, climb inside, and emerge
into the bracing frontier world of 1840, the year the last of the
original trappers rendezvous were held.

Then as now, a rendezvous offered the opportunity to visit
with old friends, purchase supplies, and have some fun with
shooting matches, trapper runs, tomahawk throws, woods walks,
and council fires. "Shinin' times," mountain men called the days
of the rendezvous.

When newcomers arrive, their clothing, shorts, sneakers, bright T-shirts, seems too electric, but within an hour they've transformed themselves. They don simple, handmade clothing of homespun cotton or soft, brain-tanned deerskin, pull on moccasins and then add the accoutrements: men stick large Bowie knives through their wide leather belts and adorn themselves with small and large leather bags, animal-claw necklaces and dangling earrings (in the left earlobe). Women don long dresses and aprons. A teenage boy pulls a wolverine mask over his head.

After the newcomers erect a tipi, they dig a fire pit and soon a good fire is blazing under the indispensable Dutch oven. Neighbors drift over and introduce themselves. The newcomers are no longer a sitcom unit, but Frontier Family Robinson.

The camp sits in a grove of tall pine trees. There are three dozen lodges—tipis painted with Indian nature symbols, or canvas tents—and the feeling is of a small village. In front of a number of these lodges blankets are spread to display handmade knives, shirts, dresses, Indian artifacts, blankets, black powder rifles, and animal skins. Traders sit by their wares and customers sit with them. Nothing is rushed.

What strikes me is the quiet. Hundreds of people are moving about, and the loudest sounds are those of children playing, and the big *boom* of the black-powder rifles at the firing range. There is not the scream of sirens, the farting of traffic, the hum of air conditioners, the din of Tinker Street or the miserable thunder of 42nd Street.

When a young man dressed as a Mohawk Indian passes by and I look over his brushy strip of a haircut, his leggings, moccasins and feathers, I realize, not for the last time at this rendezvous, that such attention to detail has resulted in rare authenticity. So much so that whenever the modern world breaks in—when I hear the sound of a plane, or a distant truck, or see a stick of Cutter's being applied to bare, brawny arms—the intrusion doesn't seem quite real, but an almost ominous intimation of a distant future.

In the hot still afternoon a banjo strikes up. Three men sit before a tipi picking out folk tunes and bluegrass melodies. The lively music deepens the illusion of time travel.

I sit and talk with a trader who calls himself "Peddler," admiring, as we palaver, his collection of handmade knives and carved staffs. Peddler sits naked, except for a breech clout (cloth), before his Dutch oven, eating lamb stew. His long, bushy black beard and glasses make him the Allen Ginsberg of backwoodsmen. I accept a beer, a porter made in Pennsylvania  since 1829. Although beer and food are kept in an ice chest, the cooler is covered with deerskin.

Peddler lives near Harrisburg and attends every rendezvous he can. The big event of his year is the giant Eastern Primitive Rendezvous to be held in September in Pennsylvania's Swatara State Park. Two to three thousand buckskinners are expected to participate, and Peddler will be there with his trader's blanket. He spoke of his love for wilderness and of his dislike of the all-terrain vehicles that make armored assaults on the forest in increasing numbers, and his disgust at the bright orange plastic modern hunters wear. Like anyone who loves the wilderness, he's opposed to what he believes is the current campaign of the U.S. Forest Service to decimate the nation's woodlands.

At a council meeting that night, activities are announced, including a scavenger hunt for the kids and a tomahawk throw. Afterwards, there's to be some singin'.

Using my flashlight as little as possible, I walk into a soft focus John Ford movie. The effect of flickering campfires and soft lantern light against the white lodges is magical. People in buckskin sit around their fires visiting with each other, sharing liquor poured from small kegs into tin cups. The feeling of community and peacefulness is palpable.

I hear a banjo playing and find a bearded man singing "It Takes a Worried Man." His repertoire ranges from folk tunes to the Beatles' "Rocky Raccoon," and the songs of rebel redneck David Alan Coe. People sing along or stand talking as they pass their jugs around and exchange mild insults and practical advice on primitive technology. The men curse regularly, but not colorfully. They will knock back a few, but they don't roar like grizzlies, as mountain men did one hundred and fifty years ago at their once a year get-togethers. Buckskinning is a family phenomenon now.

On the way back to my blanket, stumbling in the darkness, I switch on my flashlight again and a soft voice calls out, "Now would Jeremiah Johnson use a gadget like that?"

I'll bet he would have found a flashlight invaluable, but the point is, of course, that a rendezvous is a theatrical event, and I'm out of costume. The actors in the drama are dedicated to the living re-creation of history in every detail. Like many Americans, they love history, wilderness, Indian ways, simple living, family, neighborliness. Unlike others, if they can't change the modern world, for a few weeks a year, they can return to what may have been a better one.

||||||||||||||||||||||||||||||||||||||||||||||||||||||||||||||||||||||||||||||||||||
In 2008 SUNY New Paltz sold the Ashokan Field Campus to a group led by the musicians Jay Ungar and Molly Mason. Now called the Ashokan Center the facility hosts educational programs, music weekends, and other events. The website is ashokancenter.org. –W.N.
||||||||||||||||||||||||||||||||||||||||||||||||||||||||||||||||||||||||||||||||||||

# A Visit with a Zen Master

Michael Perkins

IN ZEN BUDDHIST LITERATURE, one who wishes to study under a particular Zen teacher travels far, on foot, up into the mountains to the master's monastery. Upon arrival he requests admission of a gatekeeper whose job it is to test the novice's seriousness by refusing to open the gates, not once, but many times.

With this story in mind, after years of reading about Zen and years of sporadic attempts at sitting meditation, I set off on foot from my home in Glenford one hot June morning in the direction of the Zen Mountain Monastery in Mount Tremper.

Bonnie Myotai Treace, a senior monk at the monastery, had invited me to share lunch with ZMM residents, and possibly have a few words with the monastery's spiritual leader and full-time resident teacher, Sensei John Daido Loori. For one morning and afternoon, I would be that prototypical Zen student meeting the teacher in his doshinji. I was curious to learn what he might say about the relationship of this non-religion, Zen, to the religion of art.

But first I had to get there. In the heat, the rolling hills and flatlands of the Glenford-Wittenberg Road enforced their own meditation. Developers were cutting down the forest that lined the road, and increased traffic had meant increased slaughter of opossums, turtles, chipmunks, and squirrels. Once an Indian path, the road passed Yankeetown Pond, filled with water lily pads, the Wittenberg Store and Wilson State Park, where I stopped for a swim.

Fairly well fried, I arrived at the ZMM gates at the foot of Tremper Mountain with the Esopus and Beaverkill gurgling nearby. The gatekeeper I encountered was a man struggling with a large, noisy lawnmower. The grounds were well kept, but I had envisioned robed monks cutting them meticulously with scissors—all two hundred acres tended blade by blade. When the noise stopped, I walked through the gate unchallenged and headed toward a large stone building the size of a country cathedral, built as a Dominican monastery and then used as a Lutheran camp until ZMM bought the property in 1980.

At the door a tall man I recognized as Daido was talking with a woman in black. His head was shaved, his skin was dark from the sun, and he was smoking a king-sized cigarette. He wore a faded blue work shirt opened at the neck, rolled corduroys, sandals. There was a knife at his hip, and a tattoo on his right wrist. His eyes were calm. He was enjoying himself. *This is a man who knows what he's about,* I thought. *And what others are about.* We nodded. I asked for Myotai, and the woman in black took me into a large, cool eating hall to wait for her. The cook was on vacation, and Myotai was making lunch today. I sipped tea and studied some large Zen brush paintings by Zazuaki Tanahashi, who was also the translator of the thirteenth century Zen master Dogen, whose writings were often cited in Daido's weekly talks.

My reverie was interrupted by a loud crash of glass, followed by the splash of water on a stone floor. Daido stood unperturbed in the middle of the broken glass and water. The large glass jug he was trying to place in the water cooler had slipped from his hands. I thought, *Zen teachers will do anything to get your attention.*

A dozen students appeared to help him clean up. The beating of a drum called people to lunch. When Myotai emerged from the kitchen I was introduced to Daido, who shook my hand and smiled—he was missing a tooth—with the raffish charm of a Zen hermit. It was difficult to think of him in his Zen robes.

Lunch was offered at picnic tables outside with the sun beating down. To my left, I saw a huge resurrected Christ carved into the face of the building. On my right, an American flag flapped listlessly. We ate hamburgers, hot dogs, potato salad, and pasta. I thought about all the prospective students who might have stayed away because of a dislike of brown rice, and dug in. This was a Zen monastery with a softball team. A Zen monastery where the sounds of teenagers playing Frisbee and roaring about in ATVs were heard on summer afternoons.

Daido sat the head of the table patting his dog Lobo. Myotai sat across from me, a slender, intense woman with large eyes. With us at the table and at other tables were Zen students, artists all: a composer; a flutist; two visual artists; and Joy Shuko Hintz, formerly principal dancer with the Nikolais Dance Theater.

"Most of our students are practicing artists, or they at least have an art that is a major aspect of the lives," Daido explained when we began to talk about the monastery's emphasis on the arts. Daido, himself, was a renowned photographer who'd studied with Minor White. "The ten percent who don't have an art when they come soon find one. Students are trained in classical Zen arts with the ultimate objective of developing an art form for themselves. One of the reasons I moved here was because of Woodstock's history as an art colony. My intention with our arts programming is to restore the relationship between the arts and Zen that existed in Sung Dynasty China and the Kamakura Period of Japan. Then, art was coming out of the monasteries and affecting the culture. I don't mean religious iconography, but art with a spiritual basis. Art still affects the culture more profoundly than spirituality."

But what's the difference between Zen art and Western art?

"In Western art and philosophy, there is an essence. In Zen art, the self is empty."

"What students who come here are really learning is a way of using the mind," said Myotai, who'd previously taught poetry and composition at Florida State University.

What about the cultural critics, I asked Daido, who assert that Zen is an an Eastern way that cannot be followed authentically by Americans because the cultural differences are so great?

"Zen didn't come to America. It's always been here. Once you strip away the Japanese cultural aspects, I think Zen is very applicable to Americans, if not to Western culture. We're pragmatic, self-reliant. Those are the qualities that attracted Japanese Zen teachers to come to America."

After lunch a ZMM resident took me on a tour of the monastery's serenely beautiful public spaces and then up to the outlying cabins and studios clustered near a pond with a population of frogs and snapping turtles. He pointed out two A-frame houses off in the woods where ZMM artists-in-residents lived, and an outdoor chapel in the woods shared by a Buddha form set before a cross on an altar reminiscent of the Maverick Theater.

"Almost everyone who comes here thinks they will be the only one not to have done this before, but most haven't," he said. Over the years, ZMM has introduced hundreds of workshop participants to both traditional and contemporary arts. The one that caught my eye was training in kendo, the two-thousand-year-old tradition of Japanese swordsmanship. But on my walk home I settled for a poem:

> Hot road, stone in shoe,
> Horsefly circling overhead:
> Climb the hill. Don't think.

The Zen Mountain Monastery offers regular weekend workshops in both traditional arts, such as shakuhachi (bamboo flute), haiku, and chado (tea ceremony), and in contemporary arts lead by leading figures such as Meredith Monk for voice, Pat Steir for painting, and Anne Waldman and Ed Sanders for poetry. For more information, visit the website www.mro.org/zmm/.

# Bear Crazy

Will Nixon

ONLY TWICE have I seen my wife walk out on a movie. The first was *Dead Ringers,* a David Cronenberg film about identical twin gynecologists engaged in sexual gamesmanship with women unable tell them apart. Not that my wife was a Cronenberg fan the way I was for his perverse dramas, but she did have an eye for Jeremy Irons who played both brothers. When one grew jealous over a woman, spoiling the game, the movie turned creepy in typical Cronenberg fashion. The scene that drove my wife from her seat showed gynecological instruments laid out on a red tray. Not the smooth implements of modern medicine, but crude spikes and hooks worthy of a medieval torture chamber. "I'll meet you afterward in the restaurant across the street," she said. Nor could I blame her. The sick brother on screen was about to insert a metal version of a sharp-beaked turkey head into his patient. Not for the first time I was glad I didn't have to deal with gynecologists. Therapists were hard enough.

The second walkout came in 2005. By then she was no longer my wife. Almost a decade earlier, I'd left our our marriage and our midtown apartment for a Catskills log cabin. A true Manhattanite who'd never learned how to drive, she'd had no desire to leave her career in magazine publishing, her friends, or her extended family to live in a musty cabin tucked into the folds of a mountainside. Though our marriage didn't end without great sadness, we'd evolved into loyal friends. Several times a year she bussed up to the Catskills for a weekend visit. More often I saw her in the for a movie or play. On this occasion, knowing of my fascination with bears, she'd invited me to an advance screening of *Grizzly Man* at the American Museum of Natural History.

Upon moving to the mountains I'd adopted the black bear as my personal totem. For a magazine assignment, I'd profiled an art teacher from Catskill who used nature journaling for self-exploration. On a Saturday workshop in the woods below Indian Head Mountain we'd built a stick lodge out of branches, a dome that he called an Earth Womb. Huddled inside, we heard him explain his chosen identity as "Night Loon." The carved loon he held in his lap displayed the bird's stark stunning beauty: the black velvet head, beady red eyes, piano-key neck scarf, and black and white checkered cape down its back. All these bold contrasts reflected the different sides of his life. There was also the famous call of the loon, the ethereal song that sounded both haunting and enraptured. He'd filled pages in his journals with drawings and musings about what this bird might reveal about himself. Finishing his story, the teacher told us to sit alone in the woods for half an hour to choose a wild identify for ourselves.

I found a contemplative streamside spot beside a hemlock with bark-covered roots octopus-grabbing the embankment. There was a small pool and the moss-carpeted steps of a tiny waterfall, a miniature staircase leading into an invisible kingdom of nymphs and gnomes. In a moment I knew what I was. The previous evening I'd driven up from the City, skipping a friend's party in Brooklyn to work on this assignment. He'd invited us to bring poems. What I would have read was a humorous piece I'd composed about pussy willows sold in the Union Square farmer's market. But driving upstate, listening to radio rock, I'd daydreamed another party scenario. Rather than reading a witty poem about pussy willows, I'd take the room like Jim Morrison dressed in a bear hide to recite a mythical tale about a bear while a band played behind me. To hell with my life, clipped and polite. I was moving to the Catskills to be wild.

Reassembled in the Earth Womb we finger-painted each other's faces with our new identities. I turned a woman into a wolf with a black face, green eyes, and a full moon on her forehead. She painted me brown. Finished, we crawled out of the Earth Womb, birthing our new selves. Not that we took ourselves too seriously. Split between black and white Night Loon joked that he looked like a skunk. But in the coming months as I transformed from

an urbanite into a cabin dweller this exercise stayed with me. I
hung a wooden Cherokee bear mask by my door. On a group hike
I learned to identify bear claw scratches left on beech trees when
they climbed the smooth trunks for autumn nuts. My thumb and
fingers fit easily into the spread of their claws. I had the hands of
a bear, if not the nails. Twice in my first weeks I saw a bear on the
hillside a hundred feet from my cabin.

I discovered a fascinating book, *The Sacred Paw: The Bear in
Nature, Myth, and Literature* by Paul Shepard and Barry Sanders,
which described the history of humanity seeing itself in bears.
"From time far older than memory, the bear has been a special
being: humanlike, yet close to the animals and hence to the source
of life. Like us, the bear stands upright on the soles of his feet,
his eyes nearly in a frontal plane. The bear moves his forelimbs
freely in their shoulder sockets, sits on his tail end, one leg folded,
like an adolescent slouched at the table, worries with moans and
sighs, courts with demonstrable affection, produces an excrement
similar to man's, snores in his sleep, spanks his children, is avid
for sweets, and has a moody, gruff, and morose side," the authors
wrote. Shamans believed bears had access to the underworld
during their long winter sleeps. In Native American tales woman
mated with bears to link the two species. Even today, children hug
teddy bears for comfort. As Paul Shepard wrote in another book,
*The Others: How Animals Made Us Human*, "When we moved

into cities we forgot the traditional stories of the bear. But as an archetypal figure underlying the forms of culture, it persists in our dreams and imagination as though some tracks were pressed into the human nervous system during the ice ages, leaving in our innermost natures a kind of preconscious expectation that Ursus' shaggy presence will give insight into human problems."

I saved up my money and bought a bear rug from a taxidermist. It turned out not to be the cape I needed to live out my Jim Morrison fantasy. A wooden plank sewn under the chin supported the head with its plastic jaw of bared teeth, so the animal skin couldn't be worn over my head. But I found a good use for my bear rug. I kept it on a table behind my desk chair. Whenever I needed a break from the computer, I swiveled around to share a moment with my ursine sidekick, my Ed McMahon, my number-one fan always eager to please with his bear smile and tiny black eyes.

Knowing of this fascination, my ex-wife invited me to *Grizzly Man*. At first the film presented Timothy Treadwell as he fancied himself, a do-it-yourself nature show host who spoke on camera as nearby grizzlies nosed about grassy meadows or splashed around streams fishing for salmon. After the initial shock of seeing deadly bears treated as casually as zoo animals, I couldn't resist the footage. In one scene Treadwell swam beside a bear in a river. In another he sounded like a sports announcer as two males stood upright to wrestle and bite. They looked eight feet tall, giants among men. Treadwell was having the time of his life. Though in his mid-forties, he looked twenty-seven with his sun-bleached Prince Valiant hair and high-voiced exuberance. Though I knew he'd be eaten by a grizzly in the end, I stirred with envy.

Why hadn't I been so bold? So free spirited? So crazy? In 1996, I'd quit married life in Manhattan for a log cabin as my life-changing adventure. But in 2001 I'd gone to Alaska for a guided trip in the Arctic National Wildlife Refuge, first backpacking, then river rafting through an expansive wilderness of bare mountains and tundra valleys that were home to migrating caribou, wolves, musk oxen, and grizzlies. The guides took those bears seriously. Our group had a shotgun. We each carried a pepper spray can with us to the bushes along with our trowel and toilet paper. We cooked thirty yards from our tents and didn't leave any food odors. We even spit toothpaste into streams. The few grizzlies we saw were far off in our binoculars, golden brown animals blended into tundra colors half a mile away. Our guides didn't want to venture any closer.

Alaska stole my heart. Not the bears, but the miniature birch trees that only grew to my thighs, the tiny Arctic wildflowers amid pincushion mosses, the ptarmigans nested between tundra hummocks, and the midnight sun that swung low but never set. Those who promoted oil drilling in the Arctic Refuge would have you believe that the region was a frozen white wasteland. Not in the summer it wasn't. It was a vast bonsai garden. Yet the wildlife was larger than life, from golden eagles soaring above valley cliffs to caribou stampeding near our tents. For the first time I sensed what the world had been like for early humans after the Ice Age.

Our guide told us that John Muir, the nineteenth century wilderness adventurer, had said that he was glad not to have visited Alaska until later in life because Alaska spoiled him for everyplace else. That certainly happened to me. For days after returning home to my cabin I couldn't shake off my funk. Not even climbing Overlook for the magnificent views spread from the Berkshires across the Hudson Valley to the Catskills could lift my spirits. For the first time, this vast green basin looked terribly infected with buildings and roads, farm fields and malls. In Alaska this same scene would have held nothing but tundra and caribou herds. Down at the old dump, a grassy rectangle cleared from the forest, the roads formed a distinctive figure, a diagram left by aliens perhaps. As I studied the figure, it revealed itself to me: a running man with a barbed penis and a matching tail. I was not happy to be home.

Fortunately, time heals. Alaska receded into memories. The Catskills reasserted themselves, not as Alaska admittedly, but as a lot wilder than Westchester or anywhere else I might have moved several hours from Manhattan. Standing on the Overlook fire tower one afternoon I watched a white hawk circle up from Lewis Hollow to ride almost motionless like a kite in the mountaintop wind, an albino-like angel reminding me of the magic still to be found in these mountains.

I don't remember the scene at which my ex-wife walked out of *Grizzly Man*. After the happy opening, the movie began exploring Treadwell's troubled psyche. Estranged from his parents. A failed Hollywood dreamer. A former drunk. And certainly misguided in his cocky belief that he had a special gift for communicating with bears. I saw enough of myself in Treadwell to forgive his failings. Not my ex-wife. She immediately spotted him as a manic-depressive. Even his happy episodes gave her the creeps. She didn't want to watch him meet the death he was asking for. Nor could I blame her. After our marriage she'd managed well for several years, but her life had then fallen apart until she'd been hospitalized for depression. Her mother had died. She'd lost jobs as the magazine industry went through turmoil. A relationship with a lawyer in Denver had ended. She'd hit bottom during the Christmas holidays. But she'd been on the mend for several years. She was in a group-therapy program that met three times a week, a commitment like a part time job. Yet, living daily with such people, she reacted with revulsion to Treadwell, an untreated case tempting fate until his inevitable death. We agreed to meet in her apartment after the movie. She squeezed past the long row of knees in the packed auditorium.

I stayed to the end. I stayed past the end for a discussion with Werner Herzog, the director, plus others, including a grizzly bear expert from the University of Montana, who was Treadwell's antithesis, a fiercely scientific rationalist who told us that no one should use a large carnivore as a personal therapist. His students did their research in Alaska from high up on platforms out of harm's way. He wore a professorial gray jacket with elbow patches. Plus he wore eyeglasses over a black eye patch, a detail no one in the auditorium could miss. We waited patiently through the discussion until he told us a story to rival Treadwell's. The professor had once been mauled by a grizzly. He expected to die within minutes, but for some reason the bear wandered off, leaving him bleeding on the ground. When he opened his eyes, the good eye that still worked stared out of his mouth, for the bear had ripped his face out of place. He feared that *Grizzly Man* might inspire other kooks to play best friend with bears.

My ex-wife nodded knowingly upon hearing me retell this story. But, to be honest, while married, I'd viewed her as the Queen of Caution to my King of Impulse. In summer she wouldn't let me venture outside until she'd coated my fair skin with suncream SPF 45. The way I'd tanned as a youth, starting with a red lobster roast, peeling, then spending the summer with a tan, horrified her. Nor was she wrong. She'd worked as a health editor for several magazines. But I felt lucky not to be with her a few days after the movie screening when, out on a hike to Huckleberry Point, what did I see fifty feet off but a black bear up to its shoulders in blueberry bushes. I wanted to run over and hug the creature. My inner Timothy Treadwell was alive and well.

Admittedly, I saw that a black bear wasn't a grizzly. If anything it resembled an extra-wide dog, a comparison my ex-wife once made. On one of her visits we'd walked along a woods road high above a brook. I stopped the moment I spotted the mother and cub not far below us. The mother charged down the slope so fast she would have tumbled if not so quick on her feet, then sprinted up the other hillside nearly as fast, an amazing feat for an animal that looked so bulky and shambling. Meanwhile, the cub bolted up our side, crossing the road twenty feet ahead of my ex-wife, who kept walking blithely along. After the cub hid in the woods, I asked my ex-wife when she had become so brave. "Oh," she replied, still unperturbed. "I wasn't wearing my glasses. I thought they were dogs." Bless her, I thought. The woman susceptible to every fear of the woods—she wore her pants legs tucked into her socks in defense against ticks—had let her experience trump the popular sensationalism about mothers and cubs.

She was right, too. Bears did have a doggishness. I'd once volunteered on a bear study project in the North Carolina mountains. Directed by graduate students we set up wire-loop foot traps camouflaged in fallen leaves. For bait we nailed cans of spoiled sardines to the trees. (If you want to lose your taste for sardines, spread bear bait.) After nearly two weeks, we got our reward when, checking our traps, we found a young bear tethered to a tree by a metal wire on its front paw. Each time it tried to run off, it almost tripped before sitting down in frustration. The poor creature seemed exasperated. It, too, might never again care for the stink of spoiled sardines.

After we retreated from sight, the grad students went to work. One distracted the bear, while another blew a sedative dart in its rump. In a few minutes the rest of us came out to help. The lead student sat with the bear's head in her lap, its eyes wrapped in a blue bandanna, while the rest of us worked like a medical team, treating the animal to a quick physical to determine its age, weight, and health. My responsibility was to insert a rectal thermometer to be sure that the animal's temperature wasn't dropping due to the sedative. I suppose I could have been the butt of a joke—try sticking that up a bear's ass—but I felt nothing but affection for the animal spread before me. With four legs splayed wide and a gray belly with sparse black hairs it resembled a big dog rolled onto its back for a tummy rub. This bear turned out to be a young female that weighed over a hundred pounds, huge for a dog but not impossible. Below her ribs her soft belly rose and fell with each breath. The grad students strapped a radio collar around her neck to track her wanderings in the months to come. I felt grateful to see a bear in such an intimate way. Not as a totem, but as a living, breathing animal lying calmly before me. I ran my fingers across her rough paw pads to learn what they felt like.

So the bear in the blueberries on the Huckleberry Point trail didn't frighten me. Plus I was lucky. I'd arrived quietly, so it hadn't raised its head from the twiggy green shrubbery. I could stare as long as I like. For all of my fascination with bears, I actually saw one in the woods once every year or two. Each time I was struck by their absolute blackness, their silence and solitude, their self-absorption in whatever they were doing. They were the antithesis of deer, those doe-eyed dancers so alert and ready to spring on their hurdler's legs, bobbing their white tails. Bears hardly had tails. Nor did they respect you with long wary stares. Their small eyes and wayward glances made them seem near-sighted, as if it was your smell that offended them. Maybe their indifference made them seem like emissaries from the wild that we couldn't domesticate. Seeing one was a rare chance to feel that frisson of my own wildness stirring in my civilized self. Little did I know I was just getting started. *Grizzly Man* would be my lucky charm.

In August I moved out to Pine Hill, a hamlet at the base of Belleayre Mountain, for three months. What could I say? City folk invaded Woodstock for the summer, so Woodstockers retreated to Pine Hill? Not hardly. The village of white houses was so quiet I became convinced we had a daytime population of less than half a dozen souls. There was a carpenter with a nail gun working on a house down the block, puncturing the lazy hum of the crickets. An older man sat in his wheelchair on his porch on main street, tracking sirens out on Route 28 or helicopters passing overhead. The friendly postal clerk knew my story within days, for we chatted whenever I picked up mail. As for me, I was glad to be out of Woodstock for a do-it-myself writer's retreat at a friend's house. Without my usual distractions I could write all day, walk in the evening, and read at night.

In Woodstock I was a road walker, taking my daily constitutional on Plochmann Lane or other sedate routes. In Pine Hill I was smack up against the mountain, and I loved it. In ten minutes I was off the roads up into the woods. Getting in better shape. Enjoying the solitude. My first evening I took the Cathedral Glen trail, a forty-five-minute walk through stately hemlocks into a beech forest and finally up to a meadow at the bottom of a ski run. Entering the clearing, I heard scratches on bark. Atop a pile of logged trees in the woods a small black bear charged along the round beam and leaped down to scamper into hiding. I couldn't believe it. Two bear sightings within days. Had I found the touch?

It got ridiculous. The next evening I chose a trail to the Belleayre ridgeline. While still on a gravel road marching up from town to the trail turnoff, I happened to look down through the scrim of hemlocks to see a bear on a parallel road below, probably making its garbage rounds of weekender houses. Not a great sighting, but it counted. In the next two months I had half a dozen more encounters. Never in my life had I enjoyed such a streak.

There was the tub-butted bear in Rochester Hollow, a relaxing streamside walk on a woods road that I discovered while staying in Pine Hill. After following the stream for a mile and a half, the grassy road curved west to pass through the foundation remains of a former estate. Down in an old pasture pen of stone walls now grown up in forest a bear ambled fifty yards ahead of me. Suddenly aware, it took off like a cannonball laundry bag to clamber over a wall and vanish, though it made a hell of a racket, seemingly snapping every branch that it touched. (I'd noticed the bear's love of loudness. Once, camped in the Adirondacks by a lean-to, I heard a bear making so much noise outside my tent that I pictured it disemboweling a rotten log to eat grubs. The next morning I saw that it had merely been ripping down plastic food bags hung by neighboring campers on low tree branches.) Minutes later, I surprised the tub-butted bear again for a repeat performance over another wall. I'd assumed that bears ran far off to escape human encounters. Maybe they weren't as intimidated as I liked to think. This one refused to run more than thirty or forty yards at a stretch, as if I was the one who should turn around, which I did when the road reached a chained gate.

On one of my favorite hikes, the four and a half mile loop over Balsam Mountain, I heard the telltale bashing in a cluster of aspens soon after starting my descent. I didn't see the bear, but saw the spindly trees thrashing as if suffering an internal hurricane. For the next mile I sporadically heard fresh bashing ahead, as if I was pushing the bear down the mountain, or it was leading me. I'll admit that its presence was unnerving. Maybe I'd gotten too casual. Every few years the papers carried news stories about people forced to shoot bears breaking into their houses. Bears were hungry animals, after all, not spirit guides.

By the bottom, thankfully, we'd gone our separate ways. At the Ryder Hollow lean-to, I browsed the log book and smiled at the forest ranger's harangue threatening to close the lean-to if campers didn't quit leaving trash. In the Adirondacks I'd learned about lean-tos and trash. The first night the bear had harvested my neighbors' bags stupidly hung on branch stubs. But the second night the bastard had gotten mine, roped thirty feet in the air from a branch the animal couldn't possibly have climbed. Yet, somehow, the thief had stolen my loot. The littered remains of one bag lay in the dirt, leaving me nothing but foil wrappers and uneaten coffee grounds. Worse, the second bag holding my $120 camping stove was gone. Thoroughly searching the area, I found half a dozen torn food bags dragged off under the trees, the litter of camping trips cut short. But my stove was nowhere to be found. Obviously, the Ryder Hollow lean-to was a bear's feeding ground.

Still, I was taken aback, moments after retuning to the trail, when a bear marched out of the forest toward the trail, as if to intersect with me. Maybe it had bad eyesight. I hoped it had bad eyesight. I stopped, hollered, and waved my arms high over my head. It glanced up and spun around to splash through a brook then vanish into the trees. I was glad to be fifteen minutes from my car, not camped out for the night.

Should I have grown scared? My next encounter was magical. A grassy road ran along the rolling terrain on Belleayre from the

trail summit clearing to the top of the ski runs. Raspberry brambles lined the roadside. Maybe the bear shit wasn't as plentiful as
cow patties, but it was obvious. So I wasn't surprised when I came
over a rise to find two bears down the road thirty feet from me.
Siblings, a family sighting. Nor did they notice me as they nibbled
berries. Finally, one reacted and smashed through the brambles
into the woods. But the other didn't show fear. It jumped onto a
tree, much like a cat leaping onto a scratching post, and posed for a
moment with its claws nailed into the rough bark and its small ears
aimed directly at me. Then it jumped off and followed the first. I
was enchanted. A come-to-life teddy bear hugging a tree.

Not until the end of my stay in Pine Hill at the end of October
did I see my final bear. By then darkness was falling much earlier,
so my walks were shorter, and I hadn't seen a bear in weeks. Driv-

ing back from Albany late one night, however, I spotted a bear far ahead under the street lamps by the post office. It crossed the road to a driveway that led behind a hotel, no doubt making its garbage rounds. Maybe I shouldn't have counted a trash bear in my streak, but I felt a nice sense of closure. Since *Grizzly Man*, I'd seen more bears in three months than in my nine years in the Catskills.

What did my streak mean? Perhaps nothing more than that luck happens. Cherish it when it does. Yet I recognized the change in myself. No longer was I that burned-out urbanite hungry for wilderness who'd chosen the bear for his log cabin totem. After three months in Pine Hill I was eager to get back to Woodstock and my friends. Perhaps these bears were fate's way of telling me that I'd adapted to mountain life. What once seemed mythic was now almost common. Yet I remembered an insight about the bear's place in the human imagination from *The Sacred Paw*.

To early humans in northern regions, the bear had the power of death and renewal, as an animal that disappeared in winter and returned in the spring. That's also the story of the Hero's Journey studied by Joseph Campbell and popularized in movies ranging from *The Wizard of Oz* to *Pulp Fiction*. In these adventures, the hero travels to the underworld, figuratively or literally, to confront death and seize the elixir of life which he or she then brings back to the regular world. Hadn't I endured my own death and renewal in leaving Manhattan for a log cabin? Was it by chance that I'd chosen the bear as my guide? Now that I had a new life I could see them as animals. Big. Black. Solitary. Mysterious. And with a boundless appetite for berries.

||||||||||||||||||||||||||||||||||||||||||||||||||||||||||||||||||||||||||||||||||||||||||||

Now that you know what I do when encountering a bear in the woods, which is to stop and gape, you may wonder what you should do. I spoke with Matthew Merchant, a bear expert at the state Department of Environmental Conservation. His answer: do what I do. Stand there and face the bear. Don't run away, for you might trigger the animal's impulse to chase after prey. Most often the bear will leave in a sprint or a walk. If it doesn't, talk to it in an assertive voice, wave your arms, clap your hands, make your dominance known. If worst comes to worse, back slowly away. Even mother bears with cubs have an exaggerated reputation for challenging people. They, too, usually make themselves scarce, giving you the opportunity to exit the area. Merchant has heard of very few bad encounters with bears in the woods. The trouble occurs around buildings where bears scavenging for trash have lost their fear of humans.

Huckleberry Point offers a sweeping view of Platte Clove and the Hudson Valley. It's also relatively flat. At the top of Platte Clove Road the parking area is a short distance up a dirt road on the north side. The trails out to the point are two and a half miles long.

Compared to the eastern Catskills the trails in the western regions may seem like the forgotten frontier. Even on weekends I've had established trails to myself. The guidebooks are your best source of information. My recommendations for easier hikes: the Rochester Hollow trailhead is a short drive up Matyas Road on the north side of Route 28 east of Pine Hill. The ruins are almost two and a half miles up the grassy road. The Cathedral Glen Trail on Belleayre Mountain doesn't have a trailhead. I always walked up from Bonnie View Avenue in Pine Hill to pass a small pond to the start of the trail in the woods. Or I followed a rail bed from Mill Street west to the same spot. But Carol and David White's *Catskill Trails* reports that I was on private land. They suggest starting at the Discovery Lodge at the Belleayre ski center. –W.N.

# OVERLOOK MOUNTAIN

# Overlook Mountain Invocation

Michael Perkins

By God, you're a fine mountain,
Overlook, dancing with your sisters
In a ring around our valley,
South Peak blue
      Against the northern sky!

Overlook, you are
Our farewell to houses!
Overlook, you are
Our entrance to heaven!

Great Overlook!
Open our eyes closed with coins—
Open our ears stuffed with traffic—
Open our hearts so long indifferent
To your geologic transcendence,
Great Overlook!

Admit us all who live at your knees
Into the ancient chambers of your
Immortal, marmoreal being,
Where we may be transformed
Into mountains ourselves,
      Great Overlook!

# The Overlook Mountain Poetry Salon

Will Nixon

NOT EVERY POET has a fire tower muse, but I do. She first visited in a composition I wrote for seventh-grade English, an enthusiastic account of a night my younger brother and I slept in a New Hampshire fire tower while on vacation from Connecticut with our parents. We'd backpacked up the mountain by ourselves, no small accomplishment for a ten and a twelve year old. In the tower cab, we met a bearded young man enjoying a summer idyll. A member of the Harvard mountaineering club, he regaled us with tales of winter derring-do, but insisted that summer camping be luxurious. He nibbled from a four-pound bag of grapes, read a scholarly paperback (one with a plain white cover and tiny print), and lounged for the afternoon seated upright in his puffy blue sleeping bag. I was impressed. The elevated life of the mountains was the elevated life of the mind. Alas, my seventh-grade English teacher didn't buy my big adventure. He graded my paper " 45" for its grammatical howlers and misspellings. He'd circled of my use of the word "kids" and in the margin written "goats?" I dismissed him, of course. Unlike most male teachers at our school he wasn't also a coach. He kept his limp hand in a black glove tucked in his jacket pocket, a handicap from childhood polio. How could he appreciate the thrill of camping out in a fire tower?

Three years later he sat beside me at a great turning point of my life. By then I'd grown to like him a lot. He'd encouraged me to read Kurt Vonnegut, *Catch 22*, and other rebellious books. After my rough start I'd done well at the school, but not as well as Judy Smith. At our ninth-grade graduation ceremony she won the prizes for best in biology, mathematics, pretty much everything. She deserved them. Once, during a winter heating outage, I'd seen her alone in the study hall huddled in her down coat dutifully tending to homework, while the rest of us took advantage of the building's chilliness to goof off. She worked harder than anyone. Yet when the prize for best composition was announced, I was stunned to hear my name. My English teacher, seated beside me, smiled; clearly, he'd chosen me for this honor. I'd come a long way from my "45." Walking to the podium to accept my award, I decided that I'd grow up to be a writer.

So I did in my roundabout way. After college I rented an apartment in Hoboken, New Jersey upstairs from the Clam Broth House, a historic institution once famous for its "Men Only" bar with clam shells littering the floor. Now it allowed women and had video games. But it still served free clam broth. Upstairs, I scraped the gummy black varnish off the wooden desk inherited from my grandfather and polished its coppery grain. Where he'd typed his weekly sermons and theology books as a minister, I sat down to write the Great American Novel. And promptly got the Great American Writer's Block, which made a misery of my twenties.

In time I found journalism, which unleashed my energies. By the early 1990's I lived in midtown Manhattan and commuted to work at an environmental magazine in Connecticut. When a contributor from Woodstock told me of a cheap getaway in the Catskills, a Zen monastery that charged weekend guests $50, my wife and I made reservations. Of course, by the time we'd paid for the bus fare plus the taxi ride up miles of dirt road, the weekend was no longer a bargain, but we had a lovely time anyway at the Japanese-like compound on a secluded lake. One afternoon I slipped off by myself to climb Balsam Lake Mountain, which had a fire tower.

At the time I had no interest in poetry. In fact, I mocked it by reading *New Yorker* poems aloud in a faux-British voice that made my wife laugh at my pretentiousness. Yet she'd recently given me the gift of Gary Snyder's *No Nature: New and Selected Poems* not because he was a poet but because he was a prominent environmentalist. In my teens I'd read Snyder along with his fellow Beats, Ginsberg and Kerouac, but now I found his poems surprisingly clear and evocative. They transported me back to my college days camping in the High Sierras. The first poem in the book, "Mid-

August at the Sourdough Mountain Lookout," captured that alpine feeling of grandeur tinged by loneliness. This poetry didn't need puzzles or artifice. Its simplicity made prose seem verbose.

On my way down from Balsam Lake Mountain I happened upon a freshly killed porcupine on the road. Having lived in the suburbs or city all my life, I'd never seen one up close and was surprised that its quills were as blond as plastic toothpicks, except at the dark tips. I decided to write a Gary Snyder-like poem to memorialize this poor creature. By the end of the afternoon I'd written half a dozen poems about small things that caught my eye around the monastery. That blocked novelist had found an escape route through poetry. What started as a whim that afternoon would in the ensuing years mature into a serious pursuit. Poetry and fire towers both.

To honor the muse, I arranged a poetry salon on Overlook Mountain with the help of the volunteer fire tower stewards who opened the tower cab and summit cabin to the public. As fate would have it, we had poetry weather, a drizzle under fog. Nonetheless, five of us gathered under five umbrellas in the parking lot with poetry books loaded in our daypacks. To launch our journey, I read a passage from Henry David Thoreau's essay, "Walking," in which the young scold writes: "We should go forth on the shortest walk, perchance, in the spirit of undying adventure, never to return,—prepared to send back our embalmed hearts only as relics to our desolate kingdoms. If you are ready to leave father and mother, and brother and sister, and wife and child and friends, and never see them again,—if you have paid your debts, and made your will, and settled all your affairs, and are a free man, then you are ready for a walk."

We smiled at such noble sentiments. Thank God we could ignore them.

Our naturalist guide, Rich Parisio, an educator at the state Department of Environmental Conservation, led us up the road, but not far before stopping beside a shrub tree that he identi-

202

fied as a striped maple. The trunk, which never grows more than a few inches thick, has green bark unlike any other tree in our region. The big goosefoot-shaped leaves are also unmistakable. In the past I've seen Rich hold up one of these leaves the size of his hand to say that the tree is also known as "Nature's Charmin." This morning he skipped the joke. Instead, he recalled his college dendrology class, when he spent a day in the field with a forester who kept sticking needles into striped maples. Asked why, the man explained that he was poisoning weeds. Thus ended Rich's interest in becoming a forester. Back in his dorm room, he wrote an ode to striped maples, one of his first poems. He went on to become an enthusiast. Several times, I've run into him in camp-grounds for poetry festivals. In true Bohemian fashion he has a cappuccino maker that works on his camp stove.

In my daypack I had my kind of coffee table book, *Poets on the Peaks*, a history with photos of Gary Snyder, Jack Kerouac, and Philip Whalen, three of the Beats who worked as fire lookouts in the Pacific Cascades in the 1950's. This volume tells the story behind "Mid-August at the Sourdough Mountain Lookout," namely, the two summers that Snyder spent in his early twenties in remote aeries watching for fires while studying Zen Buddhism, William Blake, *Walden,* and other works that shaped his poetry and thought. Brilliant in college, he used the fire lookout to give himself an advanced degree.

Jack Kerouac had a harder time with mountain solitude. In his novel, *Desolation Angels,* he described his anticipation that "When I get to the top of Desolation Peak and everybody leaves on the mules and I'm alone I will come face to face with God or Tathagata and find out once and for all what is the meaning of all this existence." Then the romantic quest collided with reality. "But instead I'd come face to face with myself, no liquor, no drugs, no chance of faking it but face to face with ole Hateful Duluoz Me." Nonetheless, he had a productive stay in 1956. He later wrote Philip Whalen that "up there in boredom and good health," he'd gotten "a real gas of mountain prose done in full bloom of snowburn and windburn and Sourdough burn."

Overlook hasn't hosted anyone famous, but it had a near miss in 1923 when the young poet Hart Crane visited friends for a few months on Plochmann Lane. In December he wrote in a letter: "Last Friday I climbed the mountain (Overlook) and called on the caretaker who lives in the house beside the ruins of the hotel. He is very anxious to leave, has been there for seven months, etc., and I am seriously thinking of taking the place myself at pay of 40 bucks per month and all expenses gratis. It would be a hard winter, perhaps a terrific experience, but I should like to keep away from the city and its scattered prostitutions for a while."

Crane didn't get the job. He returned to Manhattan, spent the mid-1920's composing "The Bridge," an epic poem about America inspired by the Brooklyn Bridge, then succumbed to his demons and jumped off a ship at thirty-two, a famous poetry suicide. During his turbulent life, Woodstock had provided one of his rare respites of happiness.

The drizzle had ended by the time we reached the summit, but the fog remained so thick that only the base of the fire tower's legs was visible. Nonetheless, Kathryn Paulsen climbed up the tower to feel the wet wind howl. She hadn't been up Overlook since the early 1980's when a lookout still manned the cabin. He'd been replaced by an airplane pilot who patrolled for fires. After a decade of neglect volunteers had restored the tower and the cabin, which the rest of us now opened, leaving our wet umbrellas out on the porch. We entered, switching on the solar-powered ceiling lights that worked fine in the overcast. A wooden building with informational posters on the walls and rattlesnake skins on the nature display table, the cabin provided a cozy retreat. Rich Parisio lit a twig fire in the cast iron stove, which, alas, was designed to burn coal, not giving much room to stoke up a blaze. Still, it was nice to hear crackling wood.

Pat Kramer, one of the chief volunteers, treated us to a surprise. She'd brought up lunch in advance. We spread a table cloth and laid out grapes, cheese and crackers, pretzels, hummus, pita bread, more than we could eat. To drink: coolers of ice tea and lemonade. Not to be outdone, John Spindler, the fire tower steward for the day, added the final touch: chocolate brownies smooth as fudge. We put to rest the myth of the starving poet.

Our only visitor arrived during lunch, a runner in shorts, gloves, green rain jacket, and ball cap. A friendly fellow, he was on his final lap up and down the mountain for the day, his routine training for hundred-mile footraces. "How long does that take?" I asked, never having met a hundred-miler before. "Last time I didn't do so well," he admitted. "Twenty-three hours." Twenty to twenty-one hours would have been respectable. Of course, I didn't take his disappointment too seriously. For me to run a hundred miles, having stopped running years ago, would take the better part of a month. Even staying awake for twenty-three hours might take me a day and a half, including naps. To top it off, he mentioned his eleven-year-old grandchild. He proved my theory that on Overlook you meet the most interesting people. Departing into the mist, he told us that in twenty minutes down at his car, he'd raise a beer in our honor. After he left we had the mountain to ourselves.

To begin our poetry circle, Rich Parisio told us about Petrarch, an Italian poet of the fourteenth century considered the first person in the Western tradition to climb a mountain for fun. On April 26, 1336, as Petrarch later wrote, he ascended Mount Ventoux in France with his brother and two servants. As a peak bagger, I was surprised by the idea that an activity that came so naturally to me was, in fact, an early Renaissance invention. But on the summit Petrarch opened St. Augustine's *Confessions* and chided himself for "admiring earthly things" rather than the higher satisfactions to be found in the soul. The man nearly killed mountain climbing the day he created it. After explaining this history, Rich read a poem by Gregory Orr about Petrarch, "One more/trapped man of the Renaissance/looking for some way out/that doesn't lead to God." In our secular age I'll admit that my reverence for fire towers may be the feeling that others have for church steeples.

I read the Gary Snyder poem that launched me into poetry. John Spindler chose a poem inspired not by the fire tower but by the hotel ruins, "Old Mansion," by John Crowe Ransom, a southern poet who lived from 1888 to 1974. In that old mansion Ransom saw the passing of an era. Pat Kramer followed with a popular favorite, "The Cremation of Sam McGee," by Robert Service, a tall tale about a gold miner frozen in the Klondike who finds a happy resting place in his cremation fire. "And there sat Sam, looking/cool and calm,/in the heart of the furnace roar;/And he wore a smile you could see a mile,/and he said: 'Please close that door./It's fine in here, but I greatly fear/you'll let in the cold and storm—/Since I left Plumtree,/down in Tennessee,/it's the first time I've been warm." Admittedly, our twig fire in the stove paled compared to Sam McGee's blaze, but I couldn't imagine a better setting to hear such lore than in a cabin with fog ghosting the windows. My prep school yearbook page shared with a friend had quoted Sam McGee.

Kathryn Paulsen hadn't brought a poem. Instead, she read her typed essay that had a yellow trail marker glued to the cover page. A year ago, after twenty years absence, she'd begun hiking again in the Catskills. Her first trip had been to the Mount Tremper fire tower. Inspired to visit all five of the Catskills towers, she chose Red Hill for her next adventure. "It was the day before Halloween," she read aloud. She reached Red Hill much later in the afternoon than she'd planned, but refused to turn around without trying. The trail was only a mile and a half long. It wasn't well trod, but she followed yellow markers. At sunset she reached the summit clearing. "A well-restored, majestic tower stood before me. Brightened by the last rays of sun, it seemed to say, 'I've been waiting for you.'" On the tower she snapped photos of the sky awash in pink light moments after the sun had slipped behind the receding rows of hills.

Starting down, she felt rewarded for her efforts. "The forest was luminous with the same warm gold that filled the sky. This is good," she thought. But halfway down she found the forest "much gloomier." She feared a dark lump up ahead might be a skunk. Fortunately, it was only her fear. But after the trail markers turned off a woods road to drop steeply through the forest, she had to stop. "I saw no markers ahead or behind, and no discernible trail beneath my feet." She zigzagged back uphill until she found a yellow marker again. After that, she proceeded cautiously from marker to marker, backtracking if what she thought was a yellow disk turned out to be lichen or a knothole. She got lost again for a minute or two. Then stuck for real. She stood beside a fallen log that had been sawed for the trail, but couldn't see the next marker anywhere. "There was fear, but it wasn't only that," she read us. "There was a sense of wonder that life can change so quickly. A little while ago I was happily taking photographs. Now I was thinking that I might have to spend a night in the forest. I had food and water, and my vest, but no hat or gloves." All that might come between her and the cold ground was "a two-dollar poncho and some dead leaves." She imagined doing jumping jacks to stay warm through the night. She vowed never again to hike without a flashlight.

She took a final chance, leaving the sawed log. Somehow on a slender tree she found the next marker. Now she was relying on luck. "I'd travel a short distance, choose the fattest tree, and if I couldn't see anything on it, I'd reach up and feel both sides of its trunk." She also pleaded aloud, "'Come on, come on. Please,' I coaxed, groping trees along the way." One yellow disk, now glued to her manuscript, fell off in her hand. "I must have thanked every tree with a marker on it," she read. "Then I had to leave each one behind, feeling as if I were diving into dark water, and not sure when or where I'd come up."

She crossed a stream she didn't remember from her hike up. "It *couldn't* be," she told us. But she continued. "No more than four or five markers later, I was startled by a ghostly appearance," she read, "like a haunted mailbox." It was the DEC registration box. She was safe. "After another marker or two, I was in the parking area, gazing with adoration at my sweet, my wonderful steel machine, my car."

Seated in the summit cabin I was riveted by Kathryn's story. The magic of a poetry salon had struck. Someone whom you barely know reads a piece that you never expected to hear. Yet what made her essay special wasn't just this evocation of fear. She continued for several more pages to describe the euphoria of being found. That night at home with her husband and daughter the ordinary seemed touched with grace. "Flannel sheets!" she thought, crawling into bed. "Never before had they felt so exquisitely cozy, so warm and safe."

Isn't life like that? The worst followed by the best. Though she hadn't described the Red Hill fire tower as her muse, I certainly heard that in her story. The beckoning tower had rewarded her with beauty, then cast her into darkness. She had to find her way out into a fresh appreciation of life. After she finished, I knew why I'd arranged this event. I'd heard what I needed to hear. Drawn by the tower we all get lost at some point in our lives, but we survive to continue our journey. That's why Kathryn had climbed the Overlook fire tower in the fog. She now had two left in her Catskills quest: the towers on Hunter and Balsam Lake Mountain.

The stove fire had burned down to its last coals. We packed up lunch leftovers, swept food scraps out the door, padlocked the cabin, grabbed our umbrellas, and started down the mountain, still cloaked in mist. In the soft light of the fog the wet leaves shone as green as could be. Someone should write a poem about that, I thought. Maybe it would be me.

The Overlook Mountain trailhead is at the top of Meads Mountain Road across the street from the KTD monastery. From the Village Green, drive north on Rock City Road, then cross through a four-way intersection to Meads Mountain Road. The trail to the fire tower is two and a half miles long.

The Catskills has five fire towers. I recommend them all. They're on Overlook, Tremper, Hunter, and Balsam Lake Mountains, and on Red Hill. Consult a guidebook for trail descriptions. —W.N.

# Magic Meadow

Will Nixon

FOR A DECADE I lived in Hoboken without strolling over to see Frank Sinatra's birthplace. "That's criminal," said Michael Perkins, who believes in pilgrimages. (He once walked from Red Hook to see Herman Melville's house in the Berkshires.) For five years I lived in midtown Manhattan without ferrying out to the Statue of Liberty. Michael remained silent. Now I'd gone a dozen years in the Catskills, half a dozen in Woodstock itself, without taking the five-minute hike out to Magic Meadow. To Michael this famous gathering ground for free spirits was "one of the most beautiful secret spots" in town. He vowed to take me there.

Why hadn't I gone on my own? After all, I fancied myself an intrepid explorer of Woodstock's trailless peaks and lost roads. Why had this mecca scared me off? It may seem odd to say so, living in Woodstock as I do, but I have a secret fear of hippies. Born in 1956, I grew up ten years too young to ride the crest of the Sixties, yet longed to catch up with the excitement. The summer before freshman year I prepared by reading a history of the SDS, *The Electric Kool-Aid Acid Test*, and other Sixties primers. Yet arriving at my college dorm I discovered that many of my fellow freshmen were engineering majors. And Gerald R. Ford supporters rather than Jimmy Carter fans. Months after I graduated, Ronald Reagan became President in a landslide. I never made it to the Revolution.

It wasn't just politics. The hippies also represented free sex, free drugs, free living. They weren't consumed from an early age by their resumes. Though I tried I didn't have that carefree gene. My mother had a drinking problem. My father had a worrying problem. And I, by my mid-twenties, had terrible writer's block. Plus, by the 1980's, when I landed in Hoboken, the Sixties were history. I played Sonic Youth or the Replacements on my stereo and donned a leather jacket to go out. When I left for the Catskills in 1996, I switched to a fleece jacket but kept the Sixties at a distance, viewing them as nostalgia promoted by Woodstock's tourist shops that I didn't share.

All of which somehow explains why I hadn't gone to Magic Meadow. Fortunately, Michael didn't share my neurosis. He'd lived through the thick of the Sixties in the East Village before moving to Woodstock in 1972. In the 1980's, working for the Woodstock Guild, he'd managed Magic Meadow, which had been given by Peter Whitehead, the son of Ralph Whitehead who founded the Byrdcliffe Arts Colony. From those years Michael had many memories: an outdoor lecture by Alf Evers, a meadow walk with the poets Ed Sanders and Antler, many weddings, a few memorials for close friends whose ashes were scattered on the grounds. Every June when the mountain laurels bloomed, he and the late Aileen Cramer mowed the meadow and collected litter. She remembered parties from the early 1960's for which people brought out an upright piano and kegs of beer. Michael was determined that I see this beloved spot. I was determined that he see it, too.

Four months earlier Michael had suffered a terrible accident on our last hike together, dislocating his shoulder after slipping on trail ice below Kaaterskill Falls. His injury was as bad as could be. Broken bones. Nerve damage. Surgery. Physical therapy. In the weeks afterwards he looked like a changed man. Once stooped but tall and light-footed, a man who seemed to have a helium bag floating inside his shoulders, he'd shrunken like a turtle carrying a heavy shell on his back. His head, pulled down by the weight of the arm sling on his neck, seemed to be sticking out of his chest. On the phone he told me, "I'd like to get together, but I can't lift my head up to see you. I spend all my time looking at my crotch." "Well," I replied. "That puts you in the company of the great American authors: Updike, Mailer, Roth." He laughed. I laughed. But it was bittersweet humor. Months of physical therapy lay ahead to restore his mobility.

On a July morning under a flawless blue sky, a rare respite in an otherwise soggy summer, I picked up Michael at his house for his first walk since the accident. His left forearm, though no longer in a sling, was wrapped in tan tape and encased between two pieces of hard white plastic that reminded me of a goalie's mask. I still found it incredible that his seemingly minor slip on the ice had done such damage. But he didn't consider his accident freakish bad luck. To the contrary, he saw it as a dodged bullet. He'd also suffered a cut on his forehead. If his shoulder hadn't caught the brunt of his fall, who knows what that blow to his head would have done. I felt heartened by his attitude. "Life is dangerous, but not serious," he said, explaining his aversion to self-pity. I was glad to be walking with him again.

We parked by a curve on MacDaniel Road a quarter mile downhill from the Overlook Mountain parking lot. The trail into the woods, though unmarked, was obvious. Proceeding with a black walking stick, Michael stepped a little unsteadily around the roots and rocks, but I lent him a hand. The path descended a short distance to stones piled like a low bridge across a little stream then climbed up out of the trees into the meadow.

It wasn't the green fairground I'd expected. It was both wilder and larger, a field of brown grasses, blue asters, and a few apple trees in the near ground, a thick green growth of goldenrod and meadowsweet stalks in the distance interspersed with large mountain laurel shrubs. Michael was taken aback. In his day Magic Meadow had resembled an unmowed Central Park lawn, a place for picnics or Frisbee. Obviously, nobody had mowed in ages. And they might not do so again. In October 2003, the Woodstock Guild sold the property to the Open Space Institute, a conservation group that has worked with the Woodstock Land Conservancy to more than double the amount of land protected in the Overlook Mountain Wild Forest. In February 2008 OSI sold the property to New York State. Now forest rangers manage the property as "Forever Wild." The town supervisor, Jeff Moran, has vowed not to lose Magic Meadow to forest, a wish surely shared by many who cherish memories of this former cow pasture that has been a key part of Woodstock's heritage at least since the 1930's when guests from the Mead's Mountain House (now the KTD monastery) walked down to pick flowers and watch sunsets. But the "Forever Wild" protection is guaranteed by the state constitution. In short, the meadow could return to its familiar role as a conflict zone.

Yes, hippies. They arrived in the Sixties. But with the passage of time they didn't leave. They became the Rainbow Family who continue to draw young people from each generation. By the 1980's the earlier folk music gatherings had given way to drumming circles. And Michael became the heavy trying to enforce the Woodstock Guild's rights and responsibilities in heated disputes between the drumming revelers and the neighbors on MacDaniel Road who were been driven crazy. He posted trees, "Play But Don't Stay," to no effect. He negotiated with Day, an amiable, avuncular representative of the Rainbow Family, but Day had little control over this anarchic tribe. Things reached a crescendo with the Harmonic Convergence in August 1987. Inspired by predictions made by Jose Arguelles in *The Mayan Factor* that the Earth was entering a fateful new era on the Mayan calendar, people celebrated around the world.

"Thousands of New Agers, from far and wide, gathered that evening at the meadow," Michael recalled. "The sun and moon and six of the eight planets were in alignment. Astrologically, it was called the 'Grand Time.' I walked up from town that night and found the meadow packed with believers. Cars were parked solid from the meadow all the way down to the rec field. It was a fantastic gathering, shadows flickering in the fire light, people praying, eating, making love—I remember thinking that it was a like a medieval fair."

It was also a public safety nightmare, since emergency vehicles had no room to drive up the road. In the aftermath the town tried to crack down by posting "No Parking" signs. The Rainbow

Family sued. Michael found himself traveling to Albany with town officials to testify in court.

All these years later, the drummers and the neighbors have made their peace. Michael and I followed a path cleared through the chest-high green plant stalks colored by the steeplebushes' pink flower spikes. The scattered mountain laurels bushed out taller than our heads, a size that surprised me, accustomed as I was to their lower thickets in the forest shade. We were in a field, certainly, with a blue sky dome overhead, but a field as dense as jungle. The path brought us up a gentle slope to a clearing with a stone fire ring at the edge of the woods. Two pilgrims, you might call them, still savored the warmth of their rust-orange sleeping bags on this shady side of the meadow that hadn't yet received direct sunlight. One remained fully cocooned. The other sat up to pet his golden lab. We nodded greetings. But Michael wanted to show me a tree hundreds of years old that had a lightning split down its trunk, which he considered the spiritual heart of the meadow. He'd helped scatter the ashes of of his late friend and fellow writer, Marco Vassi, at its base. But we couldn't walk downhill from the fire circle. Thick as thatch the goldenrod offered no trampled path. Frustrated, Michael all but cursed. Not only was he losing the meadow he'd known. He was losing access to a late friend.

Ironically, these dense plants that have overwhelmed the meadow may yet be its savior against forest. On a nature walk led by Michael Kudish, author of *The Catskills Forest: A History*, I learned that not every abandoned pasture fills up with trees. Many do, as proven by stone walls now running through woods, but some stay fields for decades, even on "Forever Wild" lands, if the goldenrods and other plants allow tree seedlings no room to get started. The Magic Meadow of today may be the meadow that will persist for the rest of our lives. Bad for picnics and Frisbee. Great for blue skies and late summer goldenrods flaunting their saffron yellow flowers.

Having been introduced to Magic Meadow, I decided to face my fear. The evening of a full moon I parked with cars lined down MacDaniel Road and crossed the meadow to the fire ring. I was early. The sun had just set. The unlit bonfire stood bunched in a skinny tipi. Folding chairs set in a half circle sat empty. Several people I recognized from Sunday afternoon drumming circles on the Village Green lingered by the instruments, including three large djun-djun drums wheeled out in a black cart. (I later learned about these instruments from Kevin Johnson who makes African drums and organizes the circles. For twenty-three years he has joined Magic Meadow gatherings. His shoulder tattoo displayed the drums, fire ring, and full moon. "This is my version of spirituality," he explained.) Given my early arrival I had time to chat with Day, who was not only a Rainbow Family elder but my barber. Like many barbers, he was good with scissors, great with stories.

"Michael Perkins and I used to be fierce enemies," Day said with an infectious grin. "I told him, 'You'll never get rid of us. We're like cockroaches!'" By his account, the Harmonic Convergence was a fantastic success, drawing thousands of celebrants who parked around town for rides up to the meadow. Afterwards, the town posted " No Parking" signs, but the Rainbow Family sued and won. "The judge declared us a religion," Day said, "The Moon Worshipers." They secured the right to hold gatherings. (For their part, Kevin Johnson later added, the drummers got rid of the drunks and the rowdies. "We used to have fights," he said. "It's a lot mellower now.")

A burly man with a white beard and a raspy smoker's voice that easily breaks into laughter, Day belonged to the Sixties generation. Nor had he repented. With a chuckle he said, "I wish I had a nickel for every tab of acid I've eaten up here. I'd be looking good!" But he wasn't nostalgic. The gift shop version of Woodstock marketed at Bethel Woods to Baby Boomers and their curious families didn't appeal to him. "They're trying to sell yesterday," he said. "This is today. I've sold more peace shirts in the past year than ever." In his

215

stories the Rainbow Family keeps renewing itself and spreading the word. The previous month's full moon circle drew two hundred people, all by word of mouth. (By the time I slipped away at 10:30 this crowd might have been as large.)

As darkness fell, the fire was lit, throwing sparks up at the sky. Several boys and girls toasted marsh mellows. Dozens of people sat on lawn chairs or blankets in a large circle, many with drums, many just listening. Day performed a Rainbow wedding for a middle-aged couple, a simple ceremony, tying their wrists together with rope. Several dedicated young drummers warmed their drum heads by the fire before returning to the ring. Day sat with his big round bass drum laid flat in front him and tapped with his padded mallets.

Not only did I not get the hippie gene, but I have no sense of rhythm. My drumming probably sounded as monotonous as a grandfather clock. But I didn't have to listen. In this circle I could be happily drowned out by true musicians. For a while, I felt impatient at how a round of drumming stumbled off to a start, rolled along for a while, then collapsed into a finish. These leader-less efforts didn't seem to get very far. But it's probably best to listen to a drumming circle as the antithesis of a marching band. It's like a flock of birds that follows a group intelligence independent of any one brain. Two hours later the full moon rose at last from behind the trees to cast pewtery light on the meadow. The drumming was thumping full bore. The haunting horn-like blast of a conch shell split the air. Dancers swayed in the fire light. Day pounded on his flat drum while improvising rhymes: "Endless poetry...It's in me...It's in you....Make it up as we go along...Every day is a different song."

As I walked out of the meadow, I lost sight of the bonfire but heard the drumming which seemed to grow tighter now that it rose out of the darkness. Drums have a power that's primal and thrilling. I felt it in my blood. I felt it in my bones. Thank God we had it in Woodstock, even if I wasn't much of a participant.

Not until I descended from the meadow into the pitch black woods did I wish for a flashlight. That little stream would be wet to stumble through in the darkness. Yet down to my left the two spots of light that I mistook for a moment as a dim flashlight beam reflected on water turned out to be a pair of candles placed by the stone crossing. How elegant and considerate. Dry footed, I climbed up to the road, having seen Magic Meadow in its glory.

||||||||||||||||||||||||||||||||||||||||||||||||||||||||||||||||||||||||||||||||||||
To reach Magic Meadow, park in the Overlook Mountain trailhead lot and walk down Mac-Daniel Road for about a quarter of a mile. The trail to the meadow is on the right on a curve before descending a straightaway.
||||||||||||||||||||||||||||||||||||||||||||||||||||||||||||||||||||||||||||||||||||

||||||||||||||||||||||||||||||||||||||||||||||||||||||||||||||||||||||||||||||||||||
The drumming circle meets from 4 to 6 p.m. on Sunday afternoons in the Village Green from spring through fall. They also gather under the full moon in Magic Meadow and on solstices and equinoxes. They provide drums for newcomers.—W.N.
||||||||||||||||||||||||||||||||||||||||||||||||||||||||||||||||||||||||||||||||||||

# The Great Cairns, Plus Coal Mines

Will Nixon

A DECADE AGO Dave Holden built a stone cairn for Lokie, "the best dog in the world," he tells me now, adjusting one of the flat rocks on top of the three-foot-tall circle of bluestones he laid over the course of a month on a quarry outcropping with one of the best views in Woodstock. Seen from here, the village seems to have sunken under green forest waves. One day while stacking stones, Dave had a vision of Lokie, named after a mischievous Norse god, frolicking in the next world. He heard her call out to him. "Hi Daddy! Don't worry about me. I'm doing fine." Now Dave shifts a rock to fit more neatly into place on the cairn. "I can't believe it," he says. "I'm getting choked up over a dog that died ten years ago."

Mountains are many things. One of them is burial grounds. When my mother died, I climbed to an exposed cliff slab on Breakneck Ridge overlooking the Hudson River north of West Point and tied a strip of red plaid from one of her favorite dresses to a juniper tree. A decade earlier, when she suffered a series of strokes that left her crippled in a nursing home, I'd sat in that same spot for what I considered my "born again" nature revelation. Though I'd been an Eagle Scout and a backpacker through college, I'd lived in Hoboken for eight years and had only returned to hiking recently. Knowing that my mother would never step outside again, I felt called upon to experience nature as deeply as I could. Though I didn't know it at the time, eight years later I'd leave the City for a Catskills log cabin. After my mother passed, I returned to that spot to scatter ashes from my wood stove in her honor. Perhaps everyone who loves the mountains has a similar story to share.

But first Dave had promised to show me Woodstock's coal mines. You didn't know that Woodstock had coal mines? Nor do most people. They receive a passing mention in Alf Evers's *Woodstock: History of an American Town* as a remnant of the early nineteenth century when people had high hopes of finding coal, gold, and silver in our mountains. For several years, Dave had explored the upper reaches of Lewis Hollow without finding the pair of caves described in the book. Finally, he met Evers at the top of Lewis Hollow Road for the historian to point up the mountainside to a particularly large pine tree that stood above Coal Mine Ledge. That was the marker that Dave needed.

In the early nineteenth century, he explains, New York City had "its first energy crisis. They'd used up all the wood in the region." The hunt for coal was on. A tiny seam in this ledge inspired miners to dig two caves in hopes the seam would expand underground. "Thank God, it didn't," Dave says. "The mountain got fucked up enough with bluestone quarries." Eastern Pennsylvania turned out to be coal country. Completed in 1828, the D&H Canal transported coal barges for seventy years from Pennsylvania to the Hudson below Kingston to be shipped downriver to New York City. Though bluestone quarries have left gouges in the Catskills, they're nothing like the tailings piles that stretch for miles through the Pennsylvania Appalachians, black rubble wastelands that don't even grow lichen or moss. In contrast, our quarries may seem like rock gardens with quiet pools and a profusion of small birch trees and bushes. Geology was kind to the Catskills.

To reach the caves, Dave leads us up former quarry roads that branch off along the hillside's natural benches. Some roads remain obvious, others have grown up with trees. A surprising amount of moss carpets some of these roads, a softness underfoot that makes me feel guilty where, in fact, bluestone carts once carved wheel ruts in the bedrock. At one spot Dave bends down to place a patch of moss recently scalped from its rock back where it belongs. "I always try to put moss back," he says. "It reroots faster than you think." A little farther up the road, we notice several small stones that have been pulled out of the moist brown ground like molars yanked from gums. A bear has been searching for grubs. But the scat we find lying on the moss is a coyote's, dog-like with tapered ends. I have to smile. The coyote, the Trickster figure of Indian lore, has chosen the prettiest patch of velvet green moss as its spot to take a shit. That kind of insouciance could do well in a Manhattan art gallery where beauty is often promoted and subverted at the same time.

At a certain spot, which has no discernible features that I can see, Dave steers us off the upper quarry road to angle up the hillside through the forest. We're blocked by a cliff wall that's ten feet tall, forcing us to backtrack for an easy way around it. Scampering up the leafy hillside for a few more minutes, we see a much taller cliff through the trees, one that's forty feet high. Reaching it, we find an embankment along the base that's easy to walk like a trail. The cliff is gray and shaggy with rock tripe, a plant like oversized burnt potato chips. But the bottom four feet of reddish rock have eroded under the cliff, creating an overhang. In his time Dave has slept under overhangs. He points to a fallen slab of roof rock lying on the ground to explain why he no longer does.

It may have taken him several years to find the caves, but now we reach them in moments. They're not what I expected, the doorless black doorways to coal mines that I've seen in Pennsylvania and Kentucky. These caves are widely arched shelters chopped out of rock. Very big igloos could be stored in each one. The first cave slopes gently down to a clear pool filled with rock chunks knocked off the roof and sides. In places we find chisel marks, inch-wide pipe holes left in the roof edges. Each water plink in the pool solemnly echoes. The air smells mildewy. Dave lays the tip of his walking pole on the ground by the wall to show me the coal seam, which resembles a smudge left by a charred stick rubbed across the greenish rock.

"That's it?" I say. "That's pathetic."

"Exactly," Dave agrees. His voice conveys the relief that the Catskills were spared the fate of coal country. In this cave the miners stopped after digging in forty feet. In the second cave nearby they quit after twenty feet, leaving a rectangular bathtub-like pool. Sitting in these exotic, semi-protected places, I decide that had I been a Neanderthal, they would have made respectable living quarters, provided the basements got pumped.

We follow Coal Mine Ledge for another ten minutes, then scramble down the hillside. Soon, we come to the discovery that impresses Dave even more than the caves, a stone wall a hundred feet long that ends at a large squarish boulder with a birch sapling standing on top. "It took me a while to realize that something extraordinary was going on here," Dave says. At first he assumed that the wall bordered a sheep pasture like the long walls that run straight up the hillside nearby. But why did this one end after a hundred feet? Why the slight bend in the middle? Why the great boulder anchoring one end? Finally, he saw that the boulder resembled a rattlesnake's head. Now he believes that this stone snake was a devotional shrine. "I saw this for two years before I figured it out," he continues. "Now imagine how it boggled my mind to find another one a hundred yards away, a mirror image."

He's absolutely right, though this wall is shorter and suffers from three rotten tree trunks fallen across its back. Nor is the large boulder quite so square. It slopes down at the nose. But whoever built these walls took advantage of the head-like boulders they had. Who were they? When did they build them? Why? Dave doesn't know. But as an amateur student of prehistory, who has a personal library of thirty to forty books about megaliths around the world, he's convinced that these stone snakes were not the result of a farmer clearing fields. No farmer would have had the spare time to lay stone structures as carefully constructed as these for his hobby.

Dave believes that these two snakes mark the upper boundary of what he calls a sacred precinct. Not far down the slope we find the first of the cairns, stones laid three feet high on a pedestal of exposed bedrock that insures they'll stand through time. He's mapped hundreds of cairns in this area. They all seem to have a piece of quartzite or hematite on the south side. Most stand by springs, the source of life.

Then we reach the first of the great cairns, a structure eighty feet long that has slumped in the middle but still stands solidly stacked at the ends. Originally, he believes, this structure housed chambers under the now collapsed stones. The bones of important people would have been laid to rest here.

"The Woodstock Valley was a funerary zone," Dave proposes, perhaps shared by the Lenape and Mahican Indian tribes. (Originally from Maine, Dave has Micmac and Western Abenaki ancestors in his diverse family heritage.) On the small hill at the Comeau, he explains, the bodies of the deceased were offered on raised platforms to the vultures. Then the bones were burned and laid in these cairns. Of course, Dave knows that he doesn't have hard and fast proof of this theory. Mice would have eaten the bones long ago. These people didn't have metal artifacts to leave interred with the dead. But he shows me his map sketched over the years which has hundreds of smaller cairns and seven great cairns up to a hundred feet long. The second one we visit is rounded like a whale's back. As we continue through the woods, noticing cairns everywhere, I can't help but believe that he's found something special. The mysteries of an earlier society stand before us, disguised as mere piles of stones.

# A Day in the Life of the Fire Tower

Will Nixon

SEVERAL SUMMERS AGO a friend invited me on an evening hike up Overlook with her officemates from IBM in Poughkeepsie to watch the full moon rise. As a volunteer fire tower steward, she had a key to the lookout booth at the top of the tower. About thirty of us walked up together, yet somehow I found myself alone in the tower when a blood-orange moon rose from the horizon. And not just one blood-orange moon, but three of them rising in tandem from the east, west, and north. I could have been on a *Star Trek* planet with three moons like identical triplets. But this wasn't science fiction. This was the booth's reflective windows casting a perfect illusion. Even better, the moons looked so close that I felt I could almost reach out and pick one like a fruit from the night sky. But I didn't. They rapidly rose out of their colors into their white selves, wafers of dust. My friend, who'd watched the moonrise from the summit cliff top with her colleagues—they called themselves "Beamers," which sounded *Star Trekkish*—climbed the tower to lock up for the night. I decided I wanted one of those keys. This place had magic.

My first summer as a volunteer steward I missed the moonrise. On my Saturdays and Sundays on the summit I had other plans come nightfall. I enjoyed the experience, though. Led by Dick Voloshen of Woodstock, the stewards had repaired and opened the fire tower to the public in 1999, then restored the ranger's cabin as well. Each summer some thirty volunteers offered to spend three days apiece on the summit, unlocking the facilities, answering questions, manning a brochure table set up by the fire tower's base. Our khaki shirts with a DEC patch on one sleeve and an American flag on the other gave us an air of authority. At quiet times we sat in our beach chairs, applied sun lotion, and watched the small clouds parade across the blue sky. They could be as lull-

223

ing as waves at the shore. At busy times we engaged in five-way conversations at the brochure table about rattlesnakes, the hotel ruins, or whatever else came up. Overlook is the most democratic of mountains, attracting everyone from first-time hikers to mountain runners. They came from Saugerties, Brooklyn, Poland, New Zealand, wherever. The most affecting to me that first summer was a blind Boy Scout from Massachusetts who'd backpacked over Twin and Indian Head Mountains with the help of his cane and the Scout fathers. Those two mountains have some of the steepest sides in the Catskills. The first night he hadn't reached their lean-to until 11 p.m. Yet he now stood at the base of the fire tower in his dark glasses and taught me a lesson. The tower crossbar that he touched with his hand had a ninety-degree fold along its length rather than being flat, which he said give the bar more strength. Already, he knew more about engineering than I ever would. Call me sentimental, but I had one of those choked-up moments when I thought that people really can overcome tremendous obstacles to lead full and satisfying lives.

The next year I volunteered on a Saturday at the end of June, the night of the full moon. This time I wouldn't miss my triple moonrise. I'd stay overnight at the ranger's cabin, a perk granted to stewards. In the parking lot I adjusted my backpack and noticed the sheer variety of people arriving at this mountain; it truly is the most diverse place in Woodstock. An old jeep had pulled in moments after I did, a rusty green off-roader with no top and a fishing net sticking up by the passenger seat. Grenades were stenciled across the rust like East Village graffiti art. Out hopped the driver, a friendly young man named Jeff in a ball cap and dark shades who was a snowboarder, kayaker, ice climber, etc. "Indoors is for sleeping," he told me. He'd come to stretch his legs before leaving in a week for snowboarding camp on Mount Hood in Oregon.

Then a spotless maroon minivan pulled in beside us. Out piled a group of young Asian Americans for an overnight backpack. These young men had short black hair spiky with gel. The parking lot was turning into a multicultural parade ground. I started up the mountain with Jeff and his black lab, leashed by a length of old climbing rope, but in ten minutes I quit trying to keep up. Back in my college days I'd undertaken bold adventures like cross-country skiing across the High Sierras, but now, almost thirty years later, I'd be happy to make it up to the ranger's cabin for the night.

Before reaching the hotel ruins I caught up with Jeff again. He'd pulled his dog tight on its leash and stood in a group of half a dozen people stopped on the gravel dirt road to stare at the edge by the grass. Nobody needs a field guide to identify a rattlesnake. There's a place in the chest that floods with panic before the mind has time to think, "Holy Shit!" At least there is in my chest. But I tried to step back from this fear to admire this animal, admittedly a challenge. The rattlesnake lay with several bends in its chunky, muscular body and crawled with stubborn slowness, as if to rub our noses in our fear. It had a greenish tint like algae and a tail that looked charred above the rattle, which stuck off at an odd angle like a broken pinkie. But a pudgy young boy in our midst wearing a red "Seneca" team shirt refused to be cowed. "If my dad was here," he said, "he'd catch that snake in a Gatorade bottle." As a Gatorade drinker, I cringed at the suggestion of a bottled snake. With its crayon colors Gatorade is weird enough already. Perhaps the snake didn't like the idea, either. It slid into the roadside plants and vanished within moments, perfectly camouflaged.

It proved to be a banner day for rattlers. As I manned the brochure table, several people showed me digital photos of a large one coiled up in the hotel ruins. Others were rattled at along the road. A snake enthusiast in a white sun hat, a teacher from Saugerties, led me across the summit clearing to flat boulders that create steps down among blueberry shrubs. These rocks had raised underbellies that offered perfect hideaways for snakes. But I'd never seen one here. Neither had he the first time he stood and studied the shrubs for ten minutes, peering into the twigs, leaves, and shadows. Finally, he'd jumped over the bushes into a grass patch. The instant he landed he'd heard a rattle and looked around to see three snakes revealed. A religious man he told me God had provided for his safety.

Rattlesnakes weren't always revered. Back at the brochure table, a man told me he'd grown up in Willow next door to Sonny Baldwin, the final Overlook fire tower observer from 1962 to 1988. In those earlier times, Baldwin drove a jeep to the tower and captured rattlers in a burlap bag. At home he'd spill the snakes on his lawn to impress the local boys, including this man, now middle aged. Afterward, Baldwin cut off the snakes' heads and ate the bodies for dinner. Nowadays, of course, rattlesnakes are protected as an endangered species. Everyone on Overlook knows they are to be feared, photographed, and left alone.

The brochure table had a festive atmosphere. People reached the summit in good moods. An older man told me that this was his second hike up Overlook since his heart attack. I sensed that in his quiet way he felt lucky to be here. Then a strapping boy trotted up from the final curve and immediately flipped open his cell phone to gaze into its blue light. I asked whom he was calling. "Forty minutes," he announced, checking the time. "My mom's best time is forty-eight minutes." Sure enough, she arrived eight minutes later, happily huffing along at her own speed, a Caribbean woman who'd recently moved to Saugerties with her son.

The best hat of the day belonged to a middle-aged man who also wore a Hawaiian shirt in deerskin colors. The soft rim of his brown cowboy hat was wildly bent in three directions like a bird with wide wings and a fanned tail doing a somersault. He'd hiked up Overlook for a very popular reason: to try to spot his house in the valley below. (Every time I'm on the summit I look for the dark clearing in the forest that is the old reservoir pond by my place on Sawkill Road.) This man had cleared a dozen trees on his ledge in Saugerties to give his house a view of Overlook. Up in the fire tower, though, he hadn't been able to find it. What's amazing in the summit's panoramic views is how the forest hides almost everything human. But this man wasn't worried. He'd taken high resolution digital photos that he'd enlarge on his computer to locate his house in the trees. He was having fun spying on himself.

Two solo mountain bikers arrived early in the afternoon. As an old school hiker dressed in my earth-tone trousers, khaki shirt, and scuffed-up boots, I found them exotic in their tight black shorts and colorful shirts, ribbed helmets and wraparound shades. They were figures from Marvel comics. The first to arrive was a gray haired man in a striped yellow jacket-like yellow and black shirt for "Team Overlook." He lay flat on his back on a picnic table in the fire tower shade for a few minutes, then left. The second biker was a young woman with orange stripes on her black sleeves. She planned to continue on the trail to Platte Clove, then descend by road to West Saugerties and circle back to Woodstock. As a reward for burning all those calories, she'd treat herself to pizza.

My favorites arrived later: the geocachers. Although I'd heard of this pursuit, a treasure hunt done with GPS devices, I'd never seen it in action until a father and son arrived at the table. In style they were the opposites of the mountain bikers. The father had a big belly and wore an Army camouflage shirt, plus he had sweaty stringy hair. The son, a young teen, wore a blue T-shirt displaying a skeleton riding a surfboard. They looked more like mall rats than outdoor buffs. In fact, as I'd learn, they had geochached in mall parking lots and almost everywhere else. But their enthusiasm was infectious. Who could resist a father and son who'd given their black lab the geocaching nickname of Sir Barks A Lot?

"We've been geocaching all day," the father said. Down at the Zena Cornfield, they'd found a canister hung in a tree; then behind the hotel ruins, they'd uncovered an ammo box. Now on the tower they hoped to find a "micro" cache, a magnetic key box originally meant for hiding a key under a car. Until this moment I hadn't known that the Overlook fire tower was a geocache site, nor I suspected did any of the other fire tower stewards. But now I also learned that I was a "muggle," one of the oblivious bystanders who don't know that geocachers are enjoying a treasure hunt all around us. I was glad to be let in on the secret, but also skeptical. Where could someone hide anything on the fire tower? The structure stood naked, every bolt exposed. I followed the father up the stairs, as he ran his hands under the railings and glimpsed under the steps. "It's tough to explain what you're doing when you're feeling up a fire tower," he joked. But he loved sharing these adventures with his son. When he reached the tower booth empty-handed, I wasn't surprised. Having climbed these stairs half a dozen times already that day, I knew they didn't hide any secrets.

Two more geocachers arrived, a couple who'd met the father and son on previous hunts. Standing around at the bottom of the tower, I enjoyed their geocaching lore. This key box, for example, had been hidden by Ript2Shreds who'd also placed one cache in Kingston that could only be reached with climbing equipment and another that required scuba gear. Suddenly, thirty minutes after starting, the son shouted "Got it!" from high in the tower. Down he came holding a hard plastic oval in his palm. The thin key drawer opened to small folded paper that everyone signed. Then the son climbed back up the tower and placed the magnetized micro cache beneath a stair step, a black button we could actually see from the ground. "He's found all three today," his father told me.

As dinnertime approached, several raindrops landed on the table brochures. I looked up to see the Titanic-sized underbelly of a dark cloud filling the sky overhead, though sunshine ruled in the distance. With the help of a retired man who'd recently moved to the area from Michigan, I moved the table into the ranger's cabin minutes before the rain unloaded. Several people waited out the storm indoors, reading the informative posters on the walls that recount the history of the Overlook hotels and the fire tower. The hotels went through three generations (and three fires) starting in 1871 and ending, really, by 1940, though the ruins stand tall today, a grand and gothic setting for the ultimate Halloween party I intend to arrange one day. The fire tower has a shorter history. It was moved here from Gallis Hill right off Route 28 in Kingston in 1950 and served its purpose until 1989. By then, the state had hired small-plane pilots to scout for fires. Nowadays, the state relies on cell phones and other methods that our net-worked society has for the public to report fires. But the former fire tower observers like Sonny Baldwin did a lot more than sit up in their lookout booths watching for smoke. They surveyed state property lines. They responded to emergencies. They served as emissaries of the great outdoors to people who visited the towers. Perhaps the Overlook volunteer fire tower stewards program has been successful because people appreciate meeting a person in a khaki shirt who makes them feel welcomed in a place that for many is a far cry from their backyard.

By 7 p.m. the rain had cleared and the crowds had left. I set up my cook stove on the picnic table across from ranger's cabin and saw a robin land on the long oak branch that shades the cabin door. It had built its nest right above the entrance. Obviously, this bird wasn't shy around people. As I prepared my ramen noodles (boiling water is the limit of my cooking ability), a young man came briskly around the bend, wearing one of those teardrop daypacks that is primarily a water bladder. Spotting my khaki shirt, he seemed hesitant. "You don't close, do you?" he asked. Parks by the Hudson River shut at dusk, he explained. I assured him the mountain was open all night. He was relieved. He'd come up for the sunset, "the best time of day." Twenty minutes later, as I finished my after-dinner tea, he returned to say that he'd seen a spectacular sunset, plus a rainbow over Saugerties like the arch of St. Louis. Like many who climb Overlook he started down feeling lifted by the grandeur and beauty, at least for awhile.

The time had come to climb the tower for the moonrise. Alone up in the lookout booth, I saw the summit clearing for the first time all day not as a hikers' picnic ground, but as a dirt and grass meadow reverting back to the wild. A rabbit hopped out to sniff and nibble. The oaks shook their green pom-poms in the breeze. Hermit thrushes sang their ethereal flute music. Down in the valleys I saw that an old adage was true: night rises from the ground up. The green tree tops still caught the light but floated in a black shadow sea. The first lights blinked on in villages and roadways. Through binoculars I impressed myself by identifying the Route 212 bridge over the Thruway in Saugerties where three cars inched along like a caterpillar. The truth is, I'm a sucker for the godly perspective from the fire tower, the sense of command over the daily world below now reduced to miniature, yet also the detachment of being unable to reach down to change anything. Perhaps because I don't attend church I find that the lookout booth is my pew, my place to let my spirit float in the airy realms between earth and sky.

Rain pattered on the roof. I turned to look west at a gray cloud like a giant barge dragging a rain net my way. But I didn't worry. This cloud would pass like the one before dinner.

It's my theory that you always meet people on Overlook, no matter what time of day or year. Sure enough, footsteps on the stairs shook all the way up the booth. After pausing several times on the landings, my visitor poked his head up into the dusky light through the open door on the floor. He nearly jumped when I said "hello." "You scared me!" he said. But he immediately turned friendly. I asked if he'd come for the moonrise, but he hadn't known about it. He'd simply driven over from a friend's weekend house in Red Hook for a late hike. His red rain parka looked new. I thought I saw a white flash in the storm cloud.

"Was that lightning?" I asked.

"That was lightning," he confirmed.

We hurried down from the tower and sat out the storm in the cabin. This hiker turned out to live in the suburban town where I'd grown up in Connecticut. The village had always been wealthy, but with the financial bonanza in the 2000's, the place had gone gaudy. The stately three-story houses of my boyhood, he explained, were being bought as "tear downs" to be replaced by McMansions crowding their yards. On Sound Beach Avenue, the leafy New England boulevard I'd bicycled countless times, there now stood a California-style stucco monstrosity. I listened to these descriptions with a mixture of sadness and awe. I knew that I'd never return to live in my hometown. I'd never make that kind of money. My life had led me to Woodstock, not Wall Street.

The trees blustered outside the door, but the thunder and lightning had passed. Though rain dripped from leaves, the night sky had cleared to display stars. My visitor headed down the mountain, while I climbed back up to the lookout booth. Towering gray vapors filled the eastern sky. The moonrise was a lost cause. Yet the booth windows still played reflective tricks. Mount Guardian, the lower hump west of Overlook, wore a crown of lights that only existed on the glass. This illusion of mountaintop houses wasn't magic to me, however. It was my fear of the future if we didn't protect the Catskills as a wilderness park.

Across the Hudson I saw something that wasn't a window trick. It was a sizzling, white dandelion throwing off red and green streamers. Fireworks! I hadn't expected them, but this was Saturday night before July 4th later in the week. Looking up and down the Hudson Valley, I saw a dozen fireworks displays, miniature explosions that glittered into red parachutes or green wigs surprisingly close to the ground. Until now, having seen fireworks from below, I'd assumed that their rockets climbed high in the sky to spread their colorful streamers like vaults across the black dome. They'd always looked huge. From the fire tower, though, they were no more than fleeting mushrooms as exquisite as jewels. Yet I enjoyed them no less. For years I'd intended to watch the fireworks from Overlook Mountain. Now, by chance, I was. To the north through binoculars I saw the fireworks red tinting the Albany Plaza. Far off in the storm I saw them bursting above hills. Then, for an instant, a lightning bridge spanned the horizon over the hills. Man and nature had combined to put on a hell of a show.

After 10 p.m., more rain drove me back to the cabin. I'd had a day to remember, hadn't I? The storm had denied me the triple moonrise, but I'd seen wonders I'd never expected. I gave thanks to Overlook as the mountain that always enlarges my feelings about the world. Then I stashed my food in a picnic cooler for safekeeping in case the cabin had mice.

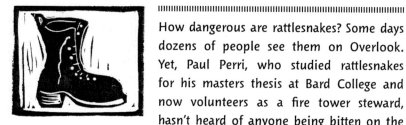

||||||||||||||||||||||||||||||||||||||||||||||||||||||||||||||||||||||||||||||||||||||||

How dangerous are rattlesnakes? Some days dozens of people see them on Overlook. Yet, Paul Perri, who studied rattlesnakes for his masters thesis at Bard College and now volunteers as a fire tower steward, hasn't heard of anyone being bitten on the mountain. Dogs run by the snakes. People make them rattle. Yet no one gets hurt because the public does the right thing, which is to stand back and watch. To get bitten, Paul says, someone needs to disturb a snake by handling it. The last bite that he knows of in our region was suffered by a farmer carrying a rattlesnake off his field in a bucket. "I've worked with experienced researchers who claim to be able to stand on rattlesnakes and not get bitten," Paul jokes. "I'm not sure I'd go that far." Yet hikers and rattlers share a peaceful coexistence on the mountain.

Nonetheless, I have heard one rattlesnake-bite story. My friend and fellow poet, Djelloul Marbrook, whom I call Del, spent his boyhood summers in Woodstock with his mother, a painter in the arts colony. During World War Two, when he was ten or so, Del was hiking down the road when he stepped over a large loose rock to be bitten above his boot by a snake coiled under the stone. "The bite didn't hurt much," he recalls, though his leg swelled like a balloon. He also felt dizzy and vomited. What hurt was the knife that his friend Woozy Dixon used to slice the puncture marks to release poison. "It was a big hunting knife, sharp as hell," Del says. "I said, 'Oh, my God, what are you doing, cutting my leg off?' He said, 'Don't whine.' I said, 'I'm not whining. Just get on with it.'" Woozy carried him to the parking lot, where they got a ride into town to the dentist, who drove Del to the hospital.

Nowadays, the first aid advice is NOT to treat a snakebite with a knife. Cutting the wound adds a new injury without removing the poison. Get the person medical care as quickly as possible. —W.N.

||||||||||||||||||||||||||||||||||||||||||||||||||||||||||||||||||||||||||||||||||||||||

# Fire Tower

Will Nixon

Never mind your replacement, the airplane.
You've pulled lightning from the sky,
tickled your legs blue with St. Elmo's fire.
You've bathed in cold fog, shed icicles
like thousands of earrings. You've whistled
through hurricanes, watched meteors
scratch the black dome in every direction
without leaving a trace. You've ignored
wars. You couldn't name a president.
You've chaperoned two generations of trees.
You've tolerated thousands of visitors
climbing the zigzag of your spine
to stand inside your empty square head
& believe they see what gods see.

# Suggestions for Further Reading

TO HIKE IN THE CATSKILLS you should use good maps and a trail guide. I recommend the New York-New Jersey Trail Conference's "Catskill Trails" map set. If you bushwhack, you'll want the USGS topographic maps.

For trail guides there are choices. My friends Carol and David White have written the Adirondack Mountain Club's *Guide to Catskill Trails*. They've also done the popular *Catskill Day Hikes for All Seasons*. Carol White edited *Catskill Peak Experiences: Mountaineering Tales of Endurance, Survival, Exploration & Adventure from the Catskill 3500 Club*, published by Black Dome Press.

The Appalachian Mountain Club publishes Peter W. Kick's *Catskill Mountain Guide*, plus his *AMC's Best Day Hikes in the Catskills and Hudson Valley*.

The Catskills own Black Dome Press offers Dick Henry's *Catskill Trails: A Ranger's Guide to the High Peaks*.

Back in the 1990's I used *Hiking the Catskills* by Lee McAllister and Myron Steven Ochman from the New York-New Jersey Trail Conference. It may no longer be in print, but I still open it fondly.

Alf Evers's *Woodstock: History of an American Town* is marvelously readable and informative. So is his magisterial *The Catskills: From Wilderness to Woodstock*.

Michael Kudish's *The Catskill Forest: A History* is an essential reference by a man who has seen as much of these mountains as anyone.

—W.N.

Poet, novelist, critic and editor, **Michael Perkins** is the author of several local histories, including *The Friends of the Library Guide to Woodstock*. He was Program Director of the Woodstock Guild for many years, and chairman of the Woodstock Bicentennial Celebration. He directs the Woodstock Library Forum, now in its twenty-fourth year.

As a poet, **Will Nixon** is the author of *My Late Mother as a Ruffed Grouse* (FootHills Publishing) plus two chapbooks *When I Had It Made* (Pudding House) and *The Fish Are Laughing* (Pavement Saw). In the past he was a freelance environmental journalist for *The Amicus Journal*, published by the Natural Resources Defense Council, *Adirondack Explorer*, and other magazines. His website is willnixon.com.

**Carol Zaloom** works primarily as a linocut illustrator. Her client list includes Random House, David Godine, HarperCollins, *Yankee* magazine, *Sky & Telescope*, the State University of New York, Bard College, and the New York City Parks Department. She lives in Saugerties.